TASTE vs. FAT

How to Save Money, Time, and Your Taste Buds by Knowing Which Brand-Name Products Rate the Highest on Taste and Nutrition

By
Elaine Magee
M.P.H., R.D.

CHRONIMED
PUBLISHING

Taste vs. Fat: Rating the Low-Fat and No-Fat Foods
© 1997 by Elaine Magee, MPH, RD.

All rights reserved. Except for brief passages for review purposes, no part of this publication may be reproduced, stored in a retrieval system, or transmitted, in any form or by any means—electronic, photocopying, recording, or otherwise—without the prior written permission of Chronimed Publishing.

Library of Congress Cataloging-in-Publication Data

Taste vs. fat / Elaine Magee
     p.   cm.
Includes index.

ISBN 1-56561-109-8 $12.95

Edited by: Jolene Steffer and Jeff Braun
Cover Design: Terry Dugan Design
Text Design & Production: David Enyeart
Art/Production Manager: Claire Lewis
Printed in the United States of America

Published by
Chronimed Publishing
P.O. Box 59032
Minneapolis, MN 55459-9686

10 9 8 7 6 5 4 3 2 1

Acknowledgments

Taste vs. Fat would not have been possible without the 18 sets of taste buds that relentlessly sampled almost every product listed in this book. Thank you for hanging in there through the good and the bad.

Lori, Chris, Anna-Celia, and Christopher Gillette

Kathy and Marc Vota

Joan, Ron, Jennifer, and Allison Redding

Steve, Mary, and Danny Sydlik

Don and Nesly Moquette

And, of course, my live-in tasters, Dennis, Devon, and Lauren Magee.

Notice: Consult a Health Care Professional

Readers are advised to seek the guidance of a licensed physician or health care professional before making changes in health care regimens, since each individual case or need may vary. This book is intended for informational purposes only and is not for use as an alternative to appropriate medical care. While every effort has been made to ensure that the information is the most current available, new research findings and product changes may invalidate some data.

Table of Contents

Introduction ... VII

Chapter 1: The Less-Fat Revolution ... 1
Fat consciousness has led to countless low-fat and no-fat products. But have we gone to extremes?

Chapter 2: Just the Fat Facts...Please! ... 7
One of the first steps to reducing the fat in your diet (and on your body) is to understand what fat is and what role it plays.

Chapter 3: Phony Bolognas: Fat Free But Full of Calories ... 19
Watch out for "light" products that are really heavy on the hogwash and fat-free products that score high on sugar and calories.

Chapter 4: All Taste Buds Are Not Created Equal ... 33
Why one food can be too sweet, too spicy, or too bitter to one person and taste perfectly fine to another.

Table of Contents

Chapter 5 Tasting Is Believing 49
The tasters: their geographic location, nutritional track record, and "motivations."

Chapter 6 The Best (and Worst) of the Light Products 59
We rate the leading low-fat and no-fat products on taste as well as nutritional attributes.

Chapter 7 Buried Treasures 177
Turn here so that you don't miss any surprising, great-tasting "diamonds in the rough."

Index 193

Taste vs. Fat

Introduction

About half of the new fat-free and light products I bring home from the supermarket end up in the garbage can. At about 3 dollars a pop that's like throwing money away. And from what I hear, I'm not the only one doing it.

Yet, if there are some diamonds in the rough, wouldn't you like to know which products those are? After all, there are thousands of light and lower-fat products on the market today; certainly some of them taste great. This handy, pocket-sized book will save you time and money by uncovering the best (and worst) of the "lights."

A handful of families (tasters) were specially selected to taste nearly every light and fat-free product on the market. They represent an assortment of taste and nutrition "motivations." For instance, some of the tasters could be described as highly health conscious, some as middle of the roaders, and others as habitual high-fat followers. The latter two are more likely to put taste and flavor at the top of their priority list.

So, how do the lower-fat and fat-free foods measure up on taste? Some score high and others way down low. Discovering which products are which is what this book is all about. Granted, you may not agree with every single rating in this book, but considering the opinions of 18 taste testers is

Introduction

better than riding roughshod through the supermarket aisles trying every new product you see, don't you think?

With a flick of the finger, you will find out which, if any, is the best tasting reduced-fat peanut butter. Are there any reduced-fat or fat-free salad dressings that you will probably like and buy again? Which microwave popcorn rates the highest in taste and nutrition? Who makes the best tasting reduced-fat vanilla creme cookie or light sausage? Which reduced-fat cheese or wheat cracker scores the highest in taste appeal? Are there any fat-free cheeses that have an acceptable taste and texture? Who makes the best tasting lower-fat vanilla and chocolate ice creams?

These are just a few of the many valuable questions answered in *Taste vs. Fat*—valuable for your health and valuable for your pocketbook.

CHAPTER ONE
The Less-Fat Revolution

Taste vs. Fat

Chapter One

Taste vs. Fat

Fat has led the pack as the consumer's top nutrition concern for six years running, according to the Food Marketing Institute. But at the same time, consumers rate taste as the top factor influencing their daily food choices, leaving nutrition, price, and even product safety in its dust.

I suspect there is a small group of people, possibly some nutritionists, bypass surgery patients, triathletes, and the like, that may rank nutrition even before taste. Perhaps that's why some of the food products favored by this group may not be very successful with the general population. Case in point: nonfat mayonnaise, rice cakes, fat-free cheese, and fat-free tortilla chips. Anyone who truly puts taste ahead of nutrition would find fault with these products. To me, eating fat-free tortilla or potato chips and rice cakes is like chewing on a piece of cardboard. Fat-free cheese is just as bad.

The Good, the Bad, and the Ugly

As with most change, changing your fat-eating habit comes with its share of pluses and minuses. And in the less-fat revolution, change has driven some people, and some products, to unhealthy and distasteful extremes. The sometimes erroneous principle, "If a little is good, more must be better," has inspired individuals and food companies alike to go a bit too far and eliminate all or most of the fat.

Many people, especially in the younger set, count grams of fat religiously—eating an almost no-fat diet. But no matter what your age, guilt is now a frequent guest at the dinner table. Many people cannot eat a fatty or even moderately fatty food without a huge dose of guilt, and guilt is not a good thing in the short or the long run.

A couple of really good things, though, have arisen from the less-fat revolution. For better or for worse, these new products give us more options when we're trying to reduce our fat intake and maintain a level of convenience. And when lower-fat foods are substituted for higher-fat foods, the percentage of calories from fat is usually reduced for the meal. The problem is, what about calories?

Fat Free, Calorie Full?

Just because a food product is fat free doesn't mean you can eat the whole box or the whole carton. This may come as a shock to some people. I think some people actually think "fat free" means no matter how much of it you eat, it won't turn to fat on your body. This would be true if not for the little matter of calories. You see, excess carbohydrate (sugar and starch) calories can turn to fat, too (although experts are still debating how much more difficult it is for your body to convert excess carbohydrate calories to body fat compared to the ease it has converting excess fat calories to body fat). And many fat-free products have the same number of calories (if not more) as their fattier versions.

According to a recent survey by the National Center for Health Statistics, fat in our diet has actually decreased from 36 percent of calories (in 1978) to 34 percent (in 1990). But here's the kicker—Americans were also found to be consuming 231 more calories per person per day. Some researchers argue that Americans are actually eating more calories due to all the fat-free and light products on the market. How can this be? There are probably many factors that are feeding this resultant rise in total calories. One could be that many of these fat-free products have just as many calories (sometimes more) as the regular versions. (Read more about this on page 21.) Another factor could be that we tend to eat more of these fat-free products compared to the regular versions.

Why do some people need to eat so much of these fat-free foods? Could it be, perhaps, that these foods are less satisfying, so they eat more in hopes of becoming more satisfied? Just a thought. Perhaps we also tend to eat more because we think they can do no harm no matter what the quantity.

Mind Over Matter

How does thinking we are eating something very low fat or fat free affect our overall intake? In one study, women were given an appetizer of yogurt, labeled either low fat or high fat, before eating lunch. Women ate more at lunch when they ate a yogurt labeled low fat than they did after eating the yogurt labeled high fat, even though the yogurts contained the same number of calories. Perhaps this has something to do with women paying less attention to their actual hunger and more attention to controlling their intake (allowing versus *not* allowing foods).

Don't Lose Sight of the Big Picture

I agree wholeheartedly with Penny Kris-Etherton, professor of nutrition at Penn State University, who believes that overall health depends on much more than the types and amounts of fats people consume. Total calories, protein, and carbohydrate eaten also have their roles. Too much attention on specific fatty acids, for example, can create the impression of a magic bullet and dilute the importance of the total amount of fat and the balance and variety of food.

CHAPTER TWO
Just the Fat Facts ...Please!

Taste vs. Fat

Chapter Two

Taste vs. Fat

What comes to mind when you hear the word *fat*? Not very pleasant, is it? Some people first think of fats in the bloodstream, others fats in their food. Still others think of fat on their bodies. Actually, these three distinct categories of fats often influence each other. And to get a handle on them, it helps to learn what motivates many of us to trim the fat in our food.

Body Fat Attack

One-third of Americans are overweight. That doesn't surprise most of us. But what shocked me was that data from NHANES III (the most recent of four national cross-sectional surveys conducted by the National Center for Health Statistics in 1988-1991) documented a dramatic increase of about 8 pounds in the mean body weight of U.S. adults since the last survey was conducted (1976-1980). It didn't matter which gender, age, or cultural group you looked at—weight gain still followed. It's safe to say then that the goal set by the Healthy People 2000 objectives to reduce the percentage of overweight adults to 20 percent will probably not be realized.

How can this be? Jenny Craig, Weight Watchers, Slim Fast, and other billion dollar dieting giants have been waging war against weight gain for decades now. Never before have more reduced-fat products been available to us. Getting back to the basics of weight control sheds some light on this sore subject.

As you've probably heard, one of the first questions related to weight control is, do the "calories in" equal "calories out"? That's because the net effect of excess calories (more than our current needs), even in the form of carbohydrates, is going to increase the amount of fat put into storage (body fat).

Well, we know that most Americans haven't exactly been increasing their "calories out" side of the equation. Due to a combination of modern life factors (television, long commutes, computers, etc.), Americans have become more, not less, sedentary.

What about the "calories in" portion? True, the average person ate less fat as a percentage of total calories during the NHANES III period (from 36 to 34 percent)—but the amount of total daily calories went up an average of 231 calories compared to 1976-1980. Aaah…now we're getting to the real million dollar question. Why would Americans suddenly increase their total daily calories at a time when the country has never been more obsessed with dieting and more concerned about healthy eating?

Ironically, some researchers think it is exactly this overemphasis on fat-free and low-fat foods that has contributed to the rampant weight gain. Perhaps this wave has fed the belief that if a food has little or no fat, you can have as much as you want without gaining weight. Perhaps when people eat mediocre fat-free foods, it leaves them feeling unsatisfied, so they eat more of the fat-free products, or end up eating something else in hopes of satisfying their hunger or food craving. Perhaps since a large chunk of the American population is actively dieting at any one time, they continue to ride the unfortunate roller coaster of strict dieting and obsession—deprivation—bingeing and guilt—strict dieting and obsession—over and over again. Studies show that when most people diet they eventually gain the weight back—and then some. Maybe some of these 8 pounds are the "and then some" from chronic dieters.

So What Are We Going to Do About It?

We all need to start doing three things:

Lesson #1 Stop dieting!
Lesson #2 Start exercising!
Lesson #3 Moderately reduce the fat in your diet (without increasing calories), but maintain a high level of taste and satisfaction.

Granted, Lessons 1 and 2 are easier said than done. But this book can definitely help you with Lesson 3. This book lists the food products with the highest satisfaction ratings—the products that the tasters said they would buy again—the products that the tasters liked even better than the regular fatty versions.

Chapter Two

A Defining Moment

It's easy to get confused while shopping in the trenches of your local supermarket. Each product label your eye catches inevitably hits you with countless advertising slogans and nutrition terms. Finally, the Food and Drug Administration released definitions for the nutrition terms food companies had been using on food packages for years. And here they are:

Low Fat: With the exception of milk, low fat means the product has no more than 3 grams of fat per serving.

Reduced Fat: The product contains at least 25 percent less fat (in grams) than the regular product.

Light: The product contains 50 percent less fat (in grams) than the regular product.

Fat Free: The product contains less than .5 grams of fat per serving.

The Funny Words that Move In Once the Fat Moves Out

It's the fear of the unknown that scares us the most, I think. But once you find out what some of these scary scientific words really mean—you realize their bark is worse than their bite. Some of the most common ingredients detected on low-fat and fat-free labels are described below:

Gums like guar gum or locust-bean gum are really soluble fibers, naturally found in tree bark and seeds, that hold water and form gels. They are most often used for their thickening powers. Xanthan gum and gellan gum are produced by microbes. Carrageenan alginate and agar come from seaweed.

Pectins are also soluble fibers, but they come from fruits such as citrus, apple, prune, date, and pear. They also are added to hold moisture and help thicken the food product.

Cellulose gel, microcrystalline cellulose, methylcellulose, or hydroxymethylcellulose all come from cellulose, an insoluble fiber that's found in all plants. Cellulose is chemically modified to form these different ingredients in order to hold moisture and form gels.

Whey protein is a milk protein which is processed into microparticles that feel like fat particles to the tongue.

Polydextrose and maltodextrin are examples of modified starches. Food starches from corn, potatoes, or tapioca are chemically modified to provide the bulk of regular starch but with fewer calories.

Chapter Two

Lecithin or mono- and diglycerides are fat substances called emulsifiers. They are added in tiny amounts to keep mixtures smooth and well mixed.

How Fat Went from Riches to Rags

Once upon a time all that the townspeople knew about food fat was that it tasted good and kept their bodies a little padded so they could better survive the winter and periods when food was scarce. People often cooked their food in lard or shortening. They uninhibitedly spread butter on their bread, corn, and potatoes. People delighted in drinking extra rich milk. Fatty meats and sausages were considered highly desirable. Aaah, what blind bliss!

Today, needless to say, things have become a lot more complicated. Fat in food is feared; its mere presence has been known to inflict massive guilt on people. At the very least, people have become cautious about fat in food. In a recent survey, 59 percent of the survey respondents said that low fat and low cholesterol were "very important" food qualities to them, beating low calorie and low sodium as concerns.

Most people have heard about bad cholesterol and good cholesterol. A high level of LDL-cholesterol in the blood increases the risk of fatty deposits forming in the arteries, increasing the risk of heart attack. That's how LDL has gotten its nickname as the "bad cholesterol." Elevated levels of

Taste vs. Fat

HDL-cholesterol, on the other hand, seem to have a protective effect against heart disease, which is why it is loosely called "good cholesterol."

Where do total cholesterol levels in the blood fit into the picture? Many people think that lowering *food* cholesterol is the most important step toward lowering *blood* cholesterol. Actually, eating less saturated fat has more of an effect on lowering blood cholesterol levels. Some studies, though, have found that eating cholesterol increases the risk of heart disease even if it doesn't increase blood cholesterol levels.

Excess food fat has been associated with heart disease and some cancers, as well as ending up as excess body fat. If the first two associations weren't enough, that third one definitely helped put the nail in fat's coffin. And that, in a nutshell, is how food fat went from riches to rags.

Here are brief definitions of key fat-related ingredient and medical terms, according to *FDA Consumer:*

Cholesterol: A chemical compound manufactured in the body. It is used to build cell membranes and brain and nerve tissues. Cholesterol also helps the body make steroid hormones and bile acids. All the cholesterol the body needs is made by the liver.

Dietary cholesterol: Cholesterol found in animal products that are part of the human diet. Egg yolks, liver, meat, some shellfish, and whole-milk dairy products are all sources of dietary cholesterol.

Fatty Acid: A molecule composed mostly of carbon and hydrogen atoms. Fatty acids are the building blocks of fats.

Fat: A chemical compound containing one or more fatty acids. Fat is one of the three main constituents of food (the others are protein and carbohydrate). It is also the principal form in which energy is stored in the body.

Hydrogenated fat: A fat that has been chemically altered by the addition of hydrogen atoms (see trans fatty acid). Vegetable oil and margarine are hydrogenated fats.

Lipid: A chemical compound characterized by the fact that it is insoluble in water. Both fat and cholesterol are members of the lipid family.

Lipoprotein: A chemical compound made of fat and protein. Lipoproteins that have more fat than protein are called low-density lipoproteins (LDLs). Lipoproteins that have more protein than fat are called high-density lipoproteins (HDLs). Lipoproteins are found in the blood, where their main function is to carry cholesterol.

Taste vs. Fat

Monounsaturated fatty acid: A fatty acid that is missing one pair of hydrogen atoms in the middle of the molecule. The gap is called an "unsaturation." Monounsaturated fatty acids are found mostly in plant and sea foods.

Monounsaturated fat: A fat made of monounsaturated fatty acids. Olive oil and canola oil are monounsaturated fats. Monounsaturated fats tend to lower levels of the LDL-cholesterol ("bad" cholesterol) in the blood.

Polyunsaturated fatty acid: A fatty acid that is missing more than one pair of hydrogen atoms. Polyunsaturated fatty acids are found mostly in plant and sea foods.

Polyunsaturated fat: A fat made of polyunsaturated fatty acids. Safflower oil and corn oil are polyunsaturated fats. Polyunsaturated fats tend to lower levels of both HDL-cholesterol and LDL-cholesterol in the blood.

Saturated fatty acid: A fatty acid that has the maximum possible number of hydrogen atoms attached to every carbon atom. It is "saturated" with hydrogen atoms. Saturated fatty acids are found mostly in animal products such as meat and whole milk.

Chapter Two

Saturated fat: A fat made of saturated fatty acids. Butter and lard are saturated fats. Saturated fats tend to raise levels of LDL-cholesterol in the blood. Elevated levels of LDL-cholesterol are associated with heart disease.

Trans fatty acid: A polyunsaturated fatty acid in which some of the missing hydrogen atoms have been put back in a chemical process called hydrogenation. Trans fatty acids are byproducts of partial hydrogenation, a process in which some of the missing hydrogen atoms are put back into polyunsaturated fats such as with vegetable shortening and margarine.

CHAPTER THREE
Phony Bolognas: Fat Free But Full of Calories

Taste vs. Fat

Chapter Three

Taste vs. Fat

Fat free or reduced fat does not a perfect product make. Many lower-fat items ring up just as many calories, if not more, than their regular counterparts. In fact, we may be doing ourselves a great disservice by eating some of these fat-free or low-fat products if we eat more of them than we would normally eat.

The majority of the fat-free and lower-fat products, I found, offer us modest calorie savings compared to the regular products—an average of 10 or 20 calories per serving. Does this mean we shouldn't buy any of these products? No—this means to truly benefit from these lower-fat or fat-free products, we need to eat the same serving size as we normally would.

If we would normally eat one Pop-Tart, then we should only eat one low-fat Pop-Tart, too. If we would normally have 1/2 cup of ice cream, then we should only eat 1/2 cup of a light ice cream. This way we are assured of eating the same or fewer calories (not more) than we would usually have—but with fewer grams of fat.

To prove this point, let's make some calorie comparisons, shall we?

3 Oreo cookies = 7 grams of fat and 160 calories;
3 SnackWell's Devil's Food Cookies = 0 fat and still 150 calories = ***10-calorie savings***

Chapter Three

14 Nabisco Mini Chips Ahoy = 7 grams fat and 150 calories; **13 SnackWell's Chocolate Chip mini cookies** = 3.5 grams fat and 130 calories
= *20-calorie savings*

1/2 cup Jell-O Instant Chocolate Pudding and Pie Filling (prepared with skim milk) = 140 calories; **1/2 cup Jell-O Free Instant Chocolate Pudding and Pie Filling** (prepared with skim milk) = 140 calories
= *0-calorie savings*

Kudos Whole Grain Bars, Chocolate Chunk, 1 bar = 90 calories; **Kudos Low Fat Whole Grain Bars, Strawberry,** 1 bar = 90 calories
= *0-calorie savings*

Mrs. Richardson Butterscotch Caramel Topping, 2 Tbsp. = 130 calories; **Smuckers Fat Free Caramel Topping,** 2 Tbsp. = 130 calories
= *0-calorie savings*

Kellogg's Strawberry Pop-Tart, 1 = 200 calories; **Kellogg's Low Fat Strawberry Pop-Tart,** 1 = 190 calories
= *10-calorie savings*

Pepperidge Farm Santa Fe Oatmeal Raisin Cookie, 1 = 130 calories; **Pepperidge Farm Reduced Fat Soft Baked Oatmeal Raisin Cookie,** 1 = 120 calories
= *10-calorie savings*

Regular Fig Newtons, 2 = 110 calories;
Raspberry Fat Free Newtons, 2 = 100 calories
= *10-calorie savings*

What Goes Up When Fat Goes Down?

In light of the previous calorie comparisons, you can't help but ask, "Given that every gram of fat is equal to 9 calories—and if fat is reduced to almost nil—why are the calories almost the same?" Well, let's get back to some nutrition basics.

Calories in our food come from either fat, protein, or carbohydrate (from sugars or starches). So, if the fat is going down, and the calories are almost the same, you have only to look at the nutrition label to see what is going up. But I'll give you one guess—in most cases it's sugar, in one form or another.

Sugar, whether it comes from honey, corn syrup, brown sugar, or high fructose corn syrup, can add moisture and help tenderize bakery products. When added to foods like ice cream, it adds flavor and structure. So I'm not surprised that manufacturers have turned to sugar for assistance while developing reduced-fat and fat-free products.

Example #1— Ice Cream and Frozen Yogurt

In addition to more sugar, you will also find a little more protein and total carbohydrates in many of these products. Light and lower-fat ice creams are a perfect example of this. We'll use my family's favorite regular ice cream (Baskin Robbins 31 Mint Chip) as our standard for the nutritional content of regular ice cream.

Let's look at a few of the low-fat and fat-free choices. You'll notice the protein generally goes up from 1 to 4 grams per serving, starch carbohydrate goes up from 1 to 8 grams, and sugars go up from 1 to 14 grams, depending on the brand and flavor.

Serving Size	Calories	Fat (g)	Protein (g)	Carbo. (g)	Sugar (g)
Baskin Robbins 31 Mint Chip					
1/2 cup	170	11	2	17	16
Häagen-Dazs Fat Free Vanilla Frozen Yogurt					
1/2 cup	140	0	6	29	17
Ben & Jerry's Choc. Chip Cookie Dough Frozen Yogurt					
1/2 cup	210	3.5	5	39	30
Ben & Jerry's Low Fat Frozen Yogurt Cherry Garcia					
1/2 cup	170	3	4	31	30
Healthy Choice Turtle Fudge Cake					
1/2 cup	130	2	3	25	23
Serving Size	Calories	Fat (g)	Protein (g)	Carbo. (g)	Sugar (g)

Example #2— Reduced-Fat Cookies

If you've ever tasted some of the fat-free cookies and felt like your teeth were going to fall out from the sweetness, it may have occurred to you that while food manufacturers were busy taking out the fat, they also must have been pouring in some extra sugar. Well, I took a look at the nutrition information for some of the reduced-fat cookies available and compared it to the regular versions.

When I compared a SnackWell's packaged brownie to a Pillsbury regular-calorie brownie from a mix, the SnackWell's had more sugar and a little more protein and only 20 fewer calories compared to the Pillsbury brownie.

A fat-free Fig Newton has only 10 fewer calories than a regular Fig Newton (which, by the way, is already low in fat, so why mess with near perfection?), but contains 8 more calories from sugar (2 grams) per two-cookie serving.

Pepperidge Farms Reduced Fat Soft Oatmeal Cookie contains a few more calories than their regular fat Santa Fe Oatmeal Cookie, which is not surprising considering the reduced-fat cookie contains a few grams more sugar and a gram more protein.

There's Something They're Not Telling You

Have you ever noticed when you are reading the label of a baking mix, that they often give the Nutrition Facts information in two columns: Mix and Baked (or As Prepared). Normally they will give you two amounts of fat grams, one from the mix and one for the total amount of fat per serving after it is prepared. This is important information, since

Chapter Three

many of these mixes call for 1/3 cup of oil, or 3 eggs, or a stick of butter or margarine.

Well, several companies have started giving only the grams of fat in the mix. If you look real closely, which is what I get paid to do, you'll see a tiny asterisk next to the grams of fat. Then you look down at the very bottom of the label and in small print it reads something like this: "Amount in mix."

They do give you the percent Daily Value for grams of fat "as baked" or "as prepared," but let's face it, what does that really mean to most people. Most people just quickly scan the label until they see grams of fat. I can just picture people thinking, "Oh, goody, 4 grams of fat!" When in reality, if they follow the directions on the box, a serving has something like 9 or 13 grams of fat. That's a big difference in anyone's book. There are many examples of this confusing labeling in your local supermarket. But for now, I'll give you two specific examples.

Pillsbury Thick 'n Fudgy Cheesecake Swirl Deluxe Brownie Mix: As you can see from the label on page 27, a serving of mix contains 4.5 grams of fat. When you follow the directions on the box, adding 1/4 cup oil and 2 eggs to the mix, the grams of fat per serving increases to 8.5 grams of fat. But you don't see 8.5 grams of fat anywhere on the label, do you? If you look real hard you'll find 14 percent Daily Value for fat in the "Prepared" column. You have to do a little math to get to 8.5 grams of fat from the "14% Daily Value" given on the label.

If you look at the percent Daily Value guide at the very bottom of the label (in smaller print), you see "less than 65 grams of fat" listed for a 2,000 calorie standard intake. Now multiply 65 grams by 14 percent, and you get 9 grams fat.

Nutrition Facts

Serving Size 1/16 package (27g)
Servings Per Container 16

Amount Per Serving	Mix	Prepared
Calories	130	170
Calories from fat	40	80
	% Daily Values**	
Total Fat 4.5g*	7%	14%
Saturated Fat 1.5g	8%	13%
Cholesterol <5mg	1%	10%
Sodium 85mg	4%	4%
Total Carbohydrate 21mg	7%	7%
Dietary Fiber less than 1g	2%	2%
Sugars 14g		
Protein 1g		
Vitamin A	0%	0%
Vitamin C	0%	0%
Calcium	0%	0%
Iron	4%	4%

*Amount in dry mix
** Percent Daily Values are based on a 2,000 calorie diet. Your daily values may be higher or lower depending on you calorie needs.

		Calories	2,000	2,500
Total Fat		Less than	65g	80g
Sat Fat		Less than	20g	25g
Cholest		Less than	300 mg	300 mg
Sodium		Less than	2,400 mg	2,400 mg
Total Carb			300g	375g
Fiber			25g	30g

Calories per gram: Fat 9 • Carbohydrate 4 • Protein 4

Chapter Three

Jell-O No Bake Double Layer Lemon Dessert: As you can see from this label, a serving of mix contains 3.5 grams of fat. That sounds real good. But when you follow the directions on the box, adding 1/3 cup margarine, 2 tablespoons sugar, and 1 1/2 cups low-fat milk to the mix, the grams of fat per serving increases to 12 grams of fat. But you don't see 12

Nutrition Facts

Serving Size 1/8 package (38g)
Servings Per Container 8

Amount Per Serving	Mix	Prepared
Calories	160	260
Calories from fat	30	110
	% Daily Values**	
Total Fat 3.5g*	5%	18%
Saturated Fat 2g	11%	20%
Cholesterol 0mg	0%	1%
Sodium 270mg	11%	15%
Total Carbohydrate 30mg	10%	12%
Dietary Fiber less than 1g	2%	2%
Sugars 19g		
Protein 2g		
Vitamin A	0%	8%
Vitamin C	0%	0%
Calcium	2%	8%
Iron	2%	2%

*Amount in dry mix
** Percent Daily Values are based on a 2,000 calorie diet. Your daily values may be higher or lower depending on you calorie needs.

	Calories	2,000	2,500
Total Fat	Less than	65g	80g
Sat Fat	Less than	20g	25g
Cholest	Less than	300 mg	300 mg
Sodium	Less than	2,400 mg	2,400 mg
Total Carb		300g	375g
Fiber		25g	30g

grams of fat anywhere on the label, do you? If you look real hard you'll find 18 percent Daily Value for fat in the "Prepared" column. You have to do a little math to get to 12 grams of fat from the "18% Daily Value" given on the label.

If you look at the percent Daily Value guide at the very bottom of the label (in smaller print), you see "less than 65 grams of fat" listed for a 2,000 calorie standard intake. Now multiply 65 grams by 18 percent, and you get 12 grams fat.

It's All in a Name

We've come to rely on certain brands with diet-sounding names to steer us toward better choices where our waistlines are concerned. Weight Watchers, Lean Cuisine, Slim Fast, and Nestle Sweet Success are all music to some of our ears. But don't let those seductive names fool you. Some of these products are just as high in calories and fat as the overtly "sinful" products farther down the aisle.

In many cases what they are selling you is portion control and a pretty name. They are simply packaging a smaller serving size than another brand. One example is a Slim Fast snack bar weighing in at 28 grams with 120 calories and 4 grams of fat. In the same category you will find the Nestle Sweet Success snack bar weighing in at 33 grams with 120 calories and 4 grams of fat. Now jog just a few feet farther down the same aisle and you'll find Kudos Milk Chocolate Chip Bar and Nutter Butter Granola Bars

Chapter Three

with the same weight, calories, and fat as the Slim Fast and Nestle Sweet Success bars. Imagine that!

But at least it's not like eating a candy bar, right? Wrong. Twenty-eight grams of a Milky Way (or half of a regular-sized bar) actually contains fewer calories (118) and the same grams of fat (4 grams) as the Slim Fast and Nestle Sweet Success snack bars.

Learning Our Lesson

One lesson to be learned is to check the portion size, the grams of fat, AND the calorie content when comparing food products. You'll be relieved to know that we've included calories, serving size, grams of fat, grams of saturated fat, milligrams of cholesterol, and sugar or sodium information (depending on which is most appropriate) for every product listed in this book.

The second lesson is a bit more difficult to master. Some of us may be using these products as an excuse to overeat. I don't think we are entirely to blame here. If these products aren't as satisfying, we're probably more likely to keep on eating and eating in the hope of reaching some level of satisfaction. Also, some of the advertising has basically encouraged us to eat as much as we want—after all, it's fat free. So many of us have just been taking these advertising slogans to heart.

My advice to all of us is to only select the light and fat-free products that we truly like—that

Taste vs. Fat

taste satisfying to us. Otherwise, they aren't going to do a hill of beans for our overall health and eating enjoyment. For example, I really love Cracker Barrel Light Sharp Cheddar. It is real cheese to me. My family has Louis Rich Turkey Bacon often and none of us miss real bacon. Reduced Fat Bisquick is a staple in my house. I add a little flavor zing by using part low-fat buttermilk and part regular low-fat milk, and we don't notice a difference in our pancakes, waffles, or biscuits.

My daughters and husband love Pringles Light and Lays Reduced Fat potato chips. None of us notice the difference between a regular hot dog and Ball Park Lite Franks. Granted, they're still fairly high in fat—but they taste like the real thing to us. So when we want hot dogs or potato chips—that's what we reach for.

Chapter Three

CHAPTER FOUR
All Taste Buds Are Not Created Equal

Taste vs. Fat

Chapter Four

Taste vs. Fat

I always knew food was a personal thing, but I had no idea it was this personal. Of course, our food choices and food habits are a reflection of who we are, but who would have thought there would be such a range in food preferences? For the life of me, I couldn't imagine how anyone could like a few of the fat-free products we sampled for this book. But, lo and behold, I would see a fellow shopper with some of these products in his or her shopping cart.

Finally, I asked one friendly shopper who had two packages of fat-free Lifetime cheddar cheese in her shopping cart, "Have you tried this before?" "Did you like it?" She said she liked many of the fat-free products available. It was then that I realized why some of these products are still on the market: If you look hard enough you will find someone who likes many of the products that our survey said were "throw aways."

Even within my group of samplers, there was a bit of dissension. There were certain products that some of my tasters liked while others threw them away. Some people noticed unappealing aftertastes (negative tastes that lingered after the initial taste and flavors dissipated) in some products while others didn't. It became painfully obvious to me that all taste buds are not created equal.

You might think that a discussion on the

anatomy of taste would focus on the one part of our anatomy where the fundamental qualities of food (salt, sour, bitter, sweet, and possibly savory) are all sensed—the tongue. But what many of us don't realize is that a food's flavor, and our enjoyment of it, relies on all our senses, not just our sense of taste. Our sense of smell, for example, intensifies our tasting experience positively or negatively. The touch and texture of a food, as well as its appearance, also influence our enjoyment.

It Starts on the Tongue

Admittedly I rarely buy fat-free bakery and ice-cream products. The reason? In a word, sugar. Some of those fat-free cookies, breakfast bars, and frozen ice creams are just too sweet for my sweet tooth. They're so sweet, my teeth actually ache when I eat them. But, like millions of other Americans, I had to give those infamous fat-free Devils Food Cakes from SnackWell's a try. I ended up giving them away. They were too sweet for me. I used to think I was a freak—I mean, who actually complains that something is too sweet! But then I saw some research that explained my taste bud dilemma.

Scientists have recently found anatomical differences in people's tongues that help explain why something may taste terribly bitter or sweet to one person and may not be tasted at all by another. Some people can be categorized as "super tasters" merely on the merits of their tongue topography; their tongues are very organized with tightly clustered papillae (the bumps you can see with the naked eye that each house many taste buds) surrounded by a ring-type structure. In nontasters, the papillae are more scattered and do not have rings.

For the most part, flavors taste stronger to supertasters, which is not surprising, given they have more papillae and more taste buds than other people. A supertaster may think something tastes perfectly good while a nontaster needs more hot sauce, salt, or flavorings to taste and enjoy it. Or, on the contrary, a supertaster may find something too bitter or too sweet while a nontaster thinks it is just fine.

Only the Nose Knows for Sure

While your tongue's taste buds are responsible for perceiving the basic tastes (salt, bitter, sour, sweet, and possibly savory), it's the nose, through olfaction, or smell, that detects the flavors of specific foods. Probably the most predictable way that the nose perceives food flavors is when food odors travel to and through the nostrils and up to olfactory receptors at the top of the nose. But I bet you didn't know you were smelling your food when you were chewing your food. When you chew, volatiles (odorous, gas-like substances) are released from the food. The volatiles are pumped up to olfactory receptors located behind the bridge of the nose, due to the pressure created simply by chewing and manipulating the food in your mouth.

Chapter Four

Obviously our nose has a strong influence over what we like and don't like to eat. But what if your snuffer isn't sniffing so well? A number of studies have shown that 50 percent of people over age 65 suffer from olfactory loss; 2 of our 18 tasters are over the age of 60. Differences in nasal receptors and taste buds, though, only partially explain differences in food preferences between people.

A Discriminating Palate

I noticed that some people were more discriminating of meat and dairy products while others were much more scrupulous about bakery items. Simply put, we are each particular about different food categories for different reasons.

One big reason could be what taste researchers call "conditioning." We are conditioned at some level to prefer or dislike certain foods or certain flavors due, in part, to our personal exposure to various foods and flavors. We are also probably physiologically conditioned to prefer foods with a positive result whether it is the physical reward of concentrated calories or positive social conditioning.

My guess is, if you were raised eating a lot of meat, you will probably be particular about meat products. Or perhaps you always had real butter growing up or maybe you only had real butter on special occasions—either situation might influence how well you accept butter substitutes, for example.

Taste vs. Fat

Fat's Role in Taste and Flavors

What exactly does fat do for the taste and flavors in food? This is a very important question, especially because this is a book about tasting and rating foods that have no fat or at least less of it. Fat makes food appealing because it has good mouth feel (it feels smooth and creamy in the mouth) and it contributes to the satisfied post-meal feeling of fullness also known as "satiety."

You may also think that fat tastes good. But fat molecules are actually too big to be processed by the taste buds. What you may be tasting when you have something with fat, is impurities and volatiles mixed with that particular fat, such as with high flavor oils like olive and sesame oil, or bacon, or my personal favorite—butter. Fat is a solvent for smells that eventually make their way to the nasal receptors. Therefore, in many cases, the greater the amount of fat, the greater the "smellability" for particular flavors.

When food manufacturers reduce the fat, the easy answer is to enhance two of the four tastes we pick up from the taste buds (sour, salt, bitter, and sweet). Manufacturers increase the saltiness and sweetness by adding salt (or other sodium sources) and sweeteners. Did you ever notice how many fat-free and reduced-fat products contain more sodium or sugar per serving than the regular products?

Chapter Four

So Why Do Fried Foods Taste So Good?

Fried foods are appealing to many of us simply because they contain a lot of fat, and maybe at some basic survival level we are programmed to want fat. Volatiles in food, which we subsequently perceive as flavors, may be released in the high temperature frying process. Deep frying at high temperatures also contributes other desirable characteristics, such as a crispy texture on the outside and moist and tender on the inside, and the unique flavors that caramelization contributes.

Do We Notice When Some of the Fat is Missing?

Generally, the more fat that is taken out of a food, the more likely we are to notice it's gone. But for many foods there is that window of opportunity—the potential to lower the fat before the food or flavor is changed significantly. Look at my favorite cheese—Cracker Barrel Light Sharp Cheddar with 6 grams of fat per ounce. This cheese, which reduced the fat by one-third, works well in almost any situation. But once you start getting down toward 4 grams of fat or less per ounce, you tend to notice a big difference in flavor and texture in those cheeses.

Reduced-fat potato chips, with one-third less fat, go over just fine with most people. But reduce the fat even further (down to nil or 2 grams of fat per ounce) and people will definitely notice a difference. My family really likes two of the reduced-fat hot dogs on the market, both with 8 grams of fat per serving. But when we tasted hot dogs with no fat or a lot less fat, no one liked them. These fat-free or low-fat products probably went beyond that window of opportunity.

According to the research that has been done using a wide range of foods, our perception of fat appears to be food-specific. That's because fat imparts a wide range of characteristics to food—crunchiness to crackers and chips, moistness to cookies and cakes, tenderness and juiciness to meats. And furthermore, we are more able to detect changes in fat content in some foods over others.

In a recent study, people were able to judge the changes in the fat content of various milk samples and milk-based foods like puddings, as well as snack mixes. But changes in the fat content of chicken spreads, egg spreads, and potato dishes were more likely to go unnoticed.

What's That Awful Aftertaste?

Fat serves many functions in food and one of the most important may be helping to balance flavors. I noticed this function many years ago when I made a dip using a dry soup packet and substituting low-fat yogurt for sour cream. The saltiness and some of the other tastes seemed much stronger in the low-fat dip. I added less of the powder to help compensate for this. But what I was probably noticing back then was not an increase in sodium but an imbalance of tastes and flavors.

For instance, a recent study discussed how a reduction in fat in several food products leads to the loss of a "rounded" flavor.

All I know is when I taste fat-free salad dressings or cheeses, something definitely tastes out of balance. When the fat decreases in a food then, the undesirable imbalance of flavors may increase.

A Little Fat Goes a Long Way

Finding that window of opportunity in lowering the fat content of a particular food is where long-term success lies. In many cases we need some fat in a product to produce optimal results. For example, in the study mentioned above, the participants liked the fat-free samples for milk, pudding, potatoes, and chicken much less than the samples that contained some fat.

Perhaps even more interesting (and encouraging for dietitians) is the fact that the highest fat samples, for many of the different foods, were not necessarily the most popular. The participants liked the 25 percent fat egg mixtures that the scientists developed for use in the study better than the fat-free samples. However, they liked the 25 percent fat spread better than the 50 percent fat spread. The participants also liked the lower percent fat snack mix better than both the medium- and high-fat snack mix samples.

Taste vs. Fat

Are You a Supertaster, Nontaster, or Somewhere in Between?

Twenty-five percent of us are supertasters (almost two-thirds of which are women), 25 percent are nontasters, and the rest of us fall somewhere in between, simply defined as "tasters," according to Dr. Linda Bartoshuk, Ph.D., a professor at Yale University Medical School.

If you are a supertaster or a nontaster, you may already know who you are. Perhaps you are one to add extra hot sauce, salt, or pepper to foods that others find just fine the way they are. Perhaps you have been told numerous times that you have a sweet tooth because you tend to like foods that others find too sweet. If so, then you, my friend, may be a nontaster.

Then again, you may be the one who finds certain foods and beverages highly undesirable because they taste too bitter or too sweet. Maybe you are sensitive to the lingering bitterness of saccharin and other additives and the stinging pain of chili peppers. And, perhaps, you tend to like foods or dishes that others find bland. If so, then you, like me, are probably a supertaster.

A Day in the Life of a Supertaster

As long as I can remember, I've been a supertaster (it's a tough job but somebody's got to do it). I seek out Mexican restaurants that serve mild rice, beans, and salsa, because otherwise my mouth is in tremendous pain and I simply don't enjoy it. I skip Thai restaurants altogether because the first time I went to one I asked for the mildest dish on the menu, and I still had to chase every bite down with a full glass of water.

I've learned from experience not to buy fat-free cookies and ice-cream because the higher sugar content makes my teeth ache. I don't bother with fat-free yogurt with artificial sweetener because the aftertastes are too strong for me. And a gin and tonic tastes like gin and poison, as far as I am concerned—it's much too bitter.

My husband commented recently that a dish I had made was "on the bland side," while I thought it was full of flavor. That wasn't the first time that's happened to me, and I'm sure it won't be the last. And once when I went wine tasting I impressed the vineyard's vintner because I tasted cherry in a particular wine, a subtlety that wine novices like me are unlikely to notice (according to the vintner). Just a day in the life of a supertaster.

Supertasters Taste Fat

Just to make everything just a tad more complicated, Dr. Bartoshuk and her colleagues discovered recently that everyone perceives fat differently. You can probably guess who does a better job of detecting changes in the fat in food—supertasters.

Taste vs. Fat

Just as all taste buds are not created equal, fat perception is not equal in all people, either. Supertasters perceive fat better. But whether or not one product is liked over another because it is sensed as having more or less fat depends on who you ask. Dr. Bartoshuk suspects that men tend to view perceiving more fat as a good thing while women tend to view it as not so good.

Could it be that women have been reconditioned to dislike the presence of a lot of fat out of fear of gaining weight? How then do you explain my total disdain for chicken skin and visible fat on meat practically since birth. As the story goes, I was trimming extra fat from my meat before I was even old enough to hold a dinner knife. Perhaps I was just a nutritionist in the making.

Supertaster Women Have Lost a Sweet Tooth

Valerie Duffy, Ph.D., assistant professor at the University of Connecticut, found that supertaster women like sweets the least of the three tasting groups (nontasters, tasters, and supertasters.) What about supertaster men and nontaster women? Those two groups did exactly the opposite—they definitely favored the sweeter tastes.

Do Dieters Prefer Fat?

Whether or not we have repeatedly dieted in our past may help determine our preference for fat in food. Animal data has indicated, for example, that preferences for dietary fat may increase following repeated cycles of weight loss and weight regain.

Actually this makes a lot of sense. Perhaps our body automatically programs itself to desire fat even more following periods of food deprivation or strict dieting, which it views as a threat to survival.

Both obese and eating disorder patients usually have a history of a high level of dietary restraint in common. So I found one recent study that measured fat and sugar preferences in both groups particularly interesting. The researchers found that obese women tended to prefer the mixtures rich in fat but low in sugar, while the anorexic women liked the sweet taste but showed an aversion to the oral sensation of dietary fats.

Different Strokes for Different Folks

What all this suggests is that there are probably some fat-associated factors, such as flavor, rather than straight fat content per se, that influence our preference for foods. At the same time, don't underestimate a person's level of motivation toward health. I think maybe the woman I mentioned earlier in this chapter with the fat-free Lifetime cheese in her shopping cart liked it because she wanted to like it. Some of us put nutrition up, as a food consideration, even higher than taste. That's not me, mind you, but I've met plenty of people who do. So

Taste vs. Fat

I guess there is a place for fat-free salad dressing, margarine, and cheese. But their place is not in my kitchen.

In my opinion, certain foods simply aren't meant to be fat free or even very low in fat. For instance, you'll notice fat-free margarines are not rated in this book—that's because I unilaterally oppose them. If you take all of the fat out of a food that is mostly fat, such as mayonnaise, cheese, or butter, then what have you really got? Something other than mayonnaise, cheese, or butter—that's for sure. It's like trying to make a fat-free oil—that's a whole different animal altogether. It's not fat-free butter, it's just a new kind of yellow goop.

Perhaps lower-fat diets would be a lot more successful if we targeted foods that can withstand a modest reduction in fat without a huge loss in taste satisfaction. What manufacturers and shoppers need to find is that optimal level of fat (optimal for health and optimal for flavor) for each particular food—admittedly not an easy task.

Fortunately, a number of products have successfully hit their optimal level of fat. You'll find them listed in Chapter 6. We also mention the flaming failures, though—the primarily fat-free products that tasters tended to throw away in disgust. Perhaps the best option in the case of these foods is to just use less of the regular-fat products.

Chapter Four

CHAPTER FIVE
Tasting Is Believing

Taste vs. Fat

Chapter Five

Taste vs. Fat

This book would not have been possible if not for the tasters who tirelessly tasted every single product I threw at them—and there were hundreds. By the end of the four-month tasting process I thought they were going to batten down the hatches when they saw me coming up their front walk carrying yet another bag of food samples.

The Heroic Tasters

Each product in this book was tasted by 18 selected testers, ranging from toddlers and teens to young, middle, and older age adults. And about half of the tasters were of the male persuasion.

But what I really selected the adult tasters for was their nutritional profile and fat-free/light product track record. About half of the tasters are nutritionally motivated and had already tried some of the fat-free and light products on the market; the other half are less concerned about matters of health and nutrition and hadn't tried even one of these new products prior to becoming a taster for this book. And since smoking is yet another factor influencing how we taste our food, two of our tasters are currently smokers and two are former smokers. Smoking appears to desensitize the taste buds and possibly the flavors we are able to smell. Smokers usually require more salt, spice, and intense flavors in

Chapter Five

their food because otherwise it tastes bland to them.

What I realized while in the thick of this taste survey was that some people are more tolerant of the flavors (or lack of flavor) in certain product categories than in other categories. For example, one couple with a strong and sordid history of high-fat meats and dairy products was mostly intolerant of the lower-fat products they tasted in those categories. At the same time, they were very tolerant of the frozen entrée selections and the fat-free and reduced-fat products they tasted in the bakery categories (cookies, crackers, brownies, etc.) Whereas a couple tasters who didn't have a strong meat and dairy diet in childhood and as adults seemed much more impressed with the reduced-fat products in those categories while being a bit more discerning of the products they tasted in the bakery categories.

I also noticed that people who weren't used to consuming many processed foods were a lot more negative about the more processed products in general, such as the frozen entrées, hot dogs, and processed cheese slices, than people who frequently used these products.

Their Job Since They Chose to Accept It...

These tasters were painfully honest at all times. They knew I wanted to know exactly what they thought. They were given a form to fill out for each product. They rated their general response to

Taste vs. Fat

each product as "tasted great," "tasted good," "tasted OK," or "threw it away." And I have to admit about half were "throw always."

They were also asked if they could taste a difference between each light product and the regular version, and they were asked if they would buy each product again. The latter question, to me, says it all. Someone could think it tasted OK but honestly they wouldn't buy it again. This is helpful for you, the reader, since odds are you wouldn't buy it again either.

And the Survey Says...

I also gathered information from people who weren't in my group of tasters. I distributed a one-page survey to two groups of people: members of my Jazzercise class in Walnut Creek, California, and corporate office workers located in Minneapolis. The survey asked two questions, "Are there any light, low-fat, or fat-free products that you tried and tasted terrible?" "Are there any light, low-fat or fat-free products that you tried and really liked?" The respondents were encouraged to write down specific brand names in answering both questions.

This survey showed me that if you look hard enough, you will find someone who actually likes one of the products that everyone else is repulsed by, and you will also find someone who hates one of the products that everyone else likes. Case in point: I had just tried an all-vegetable frozen "sausage" patty (I use the word loosely) and couldn't even finish chewing my first bite because it tasted so bad. The next day I was talking to a lady in my Jazzercise class, and she mentioned the very same sausage product as something she had recently tried and surprisingly liked! The same can be said for fat-free cheese. Certainly someone must like them because they continue to be on the supermarket shelves. But I could find no one in our tasting group that rated even the best tasting fat-free cheese any higher than "OK, but wouldn't buy again."

The Tasters in a Nutshell

Below you will find a brief description of the five families that participated in the tasting survey. I tried desperately to create a sample of tasters that would bring a diversity in age, gender, healthy eating motivation, and childhood eating patterns. Admittedly, this is far from being a scientific study, but I think this casual survey encapsulates the taste reactions of a fairly balanced group of tasters.

Family #1: Fairly health conscious and had tried some of the light and fat-free products on a regular basis before the survey with mixed results. During the survey they found some products they really liked that are now staples in their kitchen. Family #1 has two toddlers and tends to be pretty picky about their food. The mother and father make food from scratch more often than not. The mother and father were raised with a traditional moderately high-fat American diet as children. No one in this family has a history of smoking.

Family #2: Fairly health conscious in that they emphasize fresh produce and other whole foods. This family includes a male teenager who appears to be equally as health conscious as the mother. They tend not to buy many processed or packaged foods and had not tried any fat-free or less-fat products prior to this survey. The mother was raised with a very disciplined, whole-food type diet while growing up, where food was regularly weighed and measured, and sugar was avoided. No one in this family has a history of smoking.

Family #3: Not health conscious. Both the father and mother were raised with a strong meat and potatoes background. Their children are in and out of the house between college and work and only now is the mother curious about lower-fat products due to an interest in shedding a few pounds. Prior to this survey no fat-free or lower-fat food products were tried or even look at seriously. The father is a regular smoker.

Family #4: Consists of two older adults, one retired and one currently working. Frozen entrées are a weekday dinner mainstay. Due to serious health matters that have arisen over the last 10 years, this

Chapter Five

couple often tries any fat-free or reduced-fat products they happen to notice in the store. The wife grew up in Europe with a diet consisting of high-fat meat and dairy while the husband grew up in the tropics with a traditional Indonesian diet emphasizing rice and vegetables. They both gave up smoking 25 years ago.

Family #5: Consists of two adults and two preteens. The mother and one of the daughters started to become more interested in healthful eating, with a focus on eating less fat, prior to this taste survey. The mother became particularly motivated when a close cousin died in his late 40s from a heart attack. Only a few products had been tried prior to the taste survey. The mother grew up in the Midwest and describes her childhood eating style as traditional American cooking without junk food, but with dessert every night. The father smokes.

Everyone learned quite a bit from this four-month marathon tasting. Most learned that they tended to like the "light" products and tended not to like the "fat-free" products. Some learned that there were certain food categories where they would rather eat the real thing less often then switch to some of the alternatives. Some people were surprised what a good job companies had done with lightening up food categories like crackers, soups, and cookies.

Taste vs. Fat

I noticed there were some "false negatives" because people were more likely not to like a lightened product if they didn't even like the regular product. Such was the case with some tasters and commercial salad dressings, Fig Newtons, frozen entrées, and some processed foods like cheese puffs.

Nevertheless, on to the ratings…

Chapter Five

CHAPTER SIX
The Best (and Worst) of the Light Products

Taste vs. Fat

Chapter Six

Wouldn't you like to know which fat-free and less-fat products most people really liked and would definitely buy again? How about knowing which products are best left on the shelf for other unsuspecting shoppers? Knowing which products fall in either category can save you money and frustration. The last thing I want people to do is to give up on eating a low-fat diet altogether because many of the products they've tried have been revolting.

Well, after tasting hundreds of fat-free and less-fat food products with five different families, I've got good news and bad news. The bad news is over half the products were considered "throw aways" by almost every taster. The good news is you can know right now which those products are just by flipping through the rest of this book. And there's more good news.

There was a 20 percent success rate for the products we tried—most of the tasters said they would buy about 20 percent of the products again. I know that sounds rather rigid, but I purposely selected some picky palates for my tasting survey. This means people who put taste first, but health and convenience second and third in a list of personal food priorities now have quite a few viable options. Twenty percent may seem small to you, but

Taste vs. Fat

20 percent of hundreds of products is actually almost a shopping cart full of food products.

Some of the products that tasted bad to some of the tasters could be considered false negatives because the tasters also admitted even the high-fat options in those particular product categories (such as bottled salad dressings or frozen entrées) taste bad to them as well.

You know who you are. If you tend not to like frozen entrées in general, then you're probably not going to like the highest rated less-fat ones any better. If you steer away from even the regular fat bottled creamy salad dressings because you think they have a plastic, synthetic taste, chances are you'll find the fat-free and low-fat creamy dressings equally as plastic tasting.

But I can tell you what the best tasting products are within each of these categories and which products people really liked and would buy again. And that, my friends, is worth its weight in gold.

Chapter Six

Bacon	Serving Size
★★★ Louis Rich 50% Less Fat Turkey Bacon	1 slice (14g)
★★ Sizzlean (pork & turkey) skillet prepared	1 slice (24g)
★★ Morningstar Farms Breakfast Strips	2 strips (16g)

Key: 4 stars=great!, 3=good, 2=OK, 1=skip it

I was off to a good start until one of the families refused to taste any turkey bacon. (I had them try Smoke Bar Beef Bacon professing to have 45 percent less fat than pork bacon. They thought it tasted good and said they would buy it again.) I have to admit I have a historical bias toward Louis Rich bacon. I tested many of the turkey bacons on the market a couple years ago and really liked Louis Rich. Since then I have perfected the technique of pan-frying them to produce melt-in-your-mouth crispy, yes crispy, turkey bacon. (For a description, see the Helpful Hint that follows.)

According to this taste survey, Louis Rich was the best tasting alternative bacon we tried. Half the tasters said they would buy it again. It also was mentioned many times by people filling out the questionnaire listing which light products they tried and liked. Tasters thought that Sizzlean, which came in second, tasted just OK. The big white pieces of pork fat in the raw strip didn't

Taste vs. Fat

Calories	Fat (g)	Saturated Fat (g)	Cholesterol (mg)	Sodium (mg)
30	2.5	0.5	10	190
45	4	1	15	210
60	4.5	0.5	0	220

appeal to me at all. And those big chunks of fat have to go somewhere, so be prepared for a lot of grease in the pan as the strips cook.

If cooked according to the preferred oven method, the Morningstar Farms Breakfast Strips vegetable and grain protein bacon will turn out crisp. Most tasters said they threw it away but a couple tasters rated it "OK." One taster commented that it looked like a doggy treat. Not surprising then, that a few of my tasters couldn't even bring themselves to try it.

Helpful Hint: If you cook Louis Rich bacon in a thick, nonstick fry pan over low heat, flipping the strips over frequently, and being careful not to let them burn, they will be crispy with a melt-in-your-mouth texture reminiscent of real bacon. Sometimes when a side is not quite done, I turn off the heat completely and let the bacon finish cooking while the fry pan cools.

Chapter Six

Brownie Mixes		Serving Size
★★★★	Betty Crocker Sweet Rewards Family Low-Fat Brownie Mix	1/18th mix
★★★	Betty Crocker regular Fudge Brownie Mix	1/18th mix
★★	SnackWell's Low Fat Fudge Brownie Mix	1/12th mix
★★	Krusteaz Fat Free Fudge Brownies	1/16th mix

Key: 4 stars=great!, 3=good, 2=OK, 1=skip it

I decided to test the different brownie mixes with my Jazzercise class. The Betty Crocker Sweet Rewards Family Low-Fat Fudge Brownie Mix was the definite favorite, with a nice flavor and a chewy brownie texture. I also tried the regular Betty Crocker Brownie Mix, following the directions for thick brownies, but made it with 1 tablespoon vegetable oil, 7 tablespoons fat-free sour cream, and 1/2 cup egg substitute to reduce the fat. The brownies turned out moist but not cakey. I would undercook it in the future for a chewier brownie. Most people in the Jazzercise taste test really liked

Taste vs. Fat

Calories	Fat (g)	Saturated Fat (g)	Cholesterol (mg)	% Calories from sugar
130	2.5	0.5	0	55%
(made with low-fat ingredients)				
156	2.8	1	0	58%
150	2.5	0.5	0	53%
120	0	0	0	60%

this brownie but liked the chewier texture of the Betty Crocker low-fat mix better.

Tasters thought the SnackWell's brownie tasted OK. Even though I followed the directions perfectly, they turned out dry and stiff around the edges of the pan. I would undercook it next time. Tasters thought the brownies were more cakey than fudgey.

About a third of the tasters thought the Krusteaz Fat Free Brownies tasted good, a third thought they tasted OK, and a third said they would throw it away.

Chapter Six

Brownies (packaged)		Serving Size
★★★	SnackWell's Chocolate Cherry Brownie Bars	1 (37g)
★★	SnackWell's Brownies	1 (37g)
★★	Pepperidge Farm Chocolate Fudge Fat Free Brownies	1 (40g)

Key: 4 stars=great!, 3=good, 2=OK, 1=skip it

Sugar is the first ingredient in SnackWell's brownies, so I'm not surprised I found it a bit too sweet. The texture was fine, though, and the taste was OK. Half the tasters thought it tasted good or great and would buy it again; the other half thought it tasted OK or threw it away. Even better, I thought, was their Chocolate Cherry Brownie that recently came out on the market. This

Taste vs. Fat

Calories	Fat (g)	Saturated Fat (g)	Cholesterol (mg)	% Calories from sugar
130	2	0.5	0	52%
130	2	0.5	0	52%
120	0	0	0	70%

variation has a better flavor than the regular SnackWell's brownie. The Pepperidge Farm brownie has an even higher percentage of calories from sugar than the SnackWell's brownie. A couple families thought the Pepperidge Farm brownie tasted good and would buy it again. The others rated it as OK or threw it away.

Chapter Six

Cake Mixes	Serving Size
★★★1/2 Sweet Rewards Fat Free Lemon Snack Cake	1/8th mix
★★ Sweet Rewards Fat Free Chocolate Snack Cake	1/8th mix
★ Sweet Rewards Fat Free Apple-Cinnamon Snack Cake	1/8th mix

Key: 4 stars=great!, 3=good, 2=OK, 1=skip it

The three Betty Crocker's Sweet Rewards fat-free snack mixes are a case of bad, better, and best. The Apple-Cinnamon Snack Cake mix is the bad one, the Chocolate Snack Cake mix is better, and the Lemon Snack Cake mix is the best. Although I found the lemon mix a little on the sweet side, it definitely tasted good. Half the tasters said they would buy it again. The other half said it tasted OK or they threw it away.

Taste vs. Fat

Calories	Fat (g)	Saturated Fat (g)	Cholesterol (mg)	% Calories from sugar
170	0	0	0	61%
160	0	0	0	52%
170	0	0	0	52%

Most tasters thought the chocolate snack cake tasted OK—a little bland. Only a few tasters said they would buy it again. The reviews only get worse for the apple-cinnamon snack cake. Half the tasters thought it tasted OK and half said they threw it away. No one said they would buy it again.

Chapter Six

Candy Bars	Serving Size
★★★ Milky Way Lite Miniatures	5 pieces (40g)

Key: 4 stars=great!, 3=good, 2=OK, 1=skip it

There actually is a reduced-fat candy bar category now, thanks to the makers of Milky Way Lite. My guess is this is the first of several lower-fat candy bars hitting the market. Don't get too excited, though, a box of raisins is still technically the better snack. But this lower-fat candy manages to have 38 percent less fat than the regular Milky Way (ounce per ounce) and 17 percent fewer calories, while tasting exactly the same.

Taste vs. Fat

Calories	Fat (g)	Saturated Fat (g)	Cholesterol (mg)	% Calories from sugar
150	5	2.5	0	59%

Most tasters thought they were good or great tasting—just like regular Milky Way bars. One family thought they tasted OK.

What's their secret, besides making the Milky Way Lite bars smaller than the regular? They use polydextrose, which helps lower fat and calories when substituted for some of the fat.

Chapter Six

Caramel Corn	Serving Size
★★★ Fat Free Cracker Jack Caramel Coated Popcorn	1 cup (1 oz)
★★★ Louise's Fat-Free Caramel Popcorn	1 oz
★★ Smart Temptations Fat Free Caramel Corn	1 oz

Key: 4 stars=great!, 3=good, 2=OK, 1=skip it

I find it interesting that the most liked caramel corn, Fat Free Cracker Jack, is the caramel corn with the lowest percentage of calories from sugar. I'm no caramel corn connoisseur, but there seem to be two types of caramel corn; caramel corn with a yellowish glaze, and caramel corn with a darker, molasses-like glaze. If you prefer the darker-coated type like regular Cracker Jack, you will probably prefer the Fat Free Cracker Jack to the other two listed above, which have the more yellowish glaze.

I must be easy to please when it comes to caramel corn because I thought all three brands

Taste vs. Fat

Calories	Fat (g)	Saturated Fat (g)	Cholesterol (mg)	% Calories from sugar
110	0	0	0	55%
100	0	0	0	68%
(American Specialty Foods, Fargo, ND)				
100	0	0	0	76%

listed here tasted good or great. Half of our tasters thought the Fat Free Cracker Jack tasted great; the rest rated it as good or OK. Half the tasters thought Louise's Fat-Free Caramel Corn tasted great or good, while the other half rated it as OK. Only two families thought the Smart Temptations Fat Free Caramel Corn tasted good (not great) while the rest of the tasters thought it tasted OK. One family threw it out because they thought it tasted too sweet (and it does contain the highest percentage of calories from sugar).

Chapter Six

Reduced-Fat Cheese & Cheese Products		Serving Size
Cheddar:		
★★★	Cracker Barrel Light Sharp Cheddar	1 oz
★★★	Kraft 1/3 Less Fat Sharp Cheddar	1 oz
American:		
★★★	Kraft Reduced Fat 2% Milk Singles	1 slice (21g)
Monterey Jack:		
★★★	Sonoma Dairies Garlic Jack 50% Less Fat	1 oz
★★★	Sonoma Dairies Lite Jack	1 oz
★★★	Kraft 1/3 Less Fat Monterey Jack	1 oz
Ricotta:		
★★★	Precious Low Fat	1/4 cup
Swiss:		
★★★	Jarlsberg Lite	1 oz
★★★	Sargento Light Swiss	1 oz
★★	Alpine Lace Reduced Fat Swiss	1 oz

Key: 4 stars=great!, 3=good, 2=OK, 1=skip it

I wasn't too surprised to see my tried and true cheddar of many years, Cracker Barrel Light Sharp Cheddar, was liked by the most tasters. After all, it still has a respectable amount of fat for a "cheese"—6 grams of fat per ounce, so it's more

Taste vs. Fat

Calories	Fat (g)	Saturated Fat (g)	Cholesterol (mg)	Sodium (mg)
90	6	4	20	240
91	6	4	18	237
50	3	2	10	330
70	4	2.5	15	180
70	4	2.5	15	180
80	5	3.5	20	220
70	3	1.5	15	45
(usually in the deli section of your supermarket)				
70	3.5	2	10	130
80	4	2.5	15	50
(in deli section)				
90	6	4	20	35

likely to look and taste like regular cheese than a cheese with more fat removed. I've been using this cheese for years and have found it works great in every cheese situation (in recipes, on crackers, and for making grilled cheese sandwiches).

Chapter Six

Reduced-Fat Cheese (continued)

Most of the tasters thought it tasted good and said they would buy it again. There was one family that thought it tasted good but wouldn't buy it again because it didn't melt as well as regular cheese. I guess I'm not that picky about how well my cheese melts—just so it does. Then again, it's been so long since I've cooked with regular cheese, I don't really recall how it melts.

Most tasters thought the Kraft 1/3 Less Fat Sharp Cheddar also had a good taste and would buy it again. There was one family that thought it tasted just OK.

If you are looking for lower-fat American singles, Kraft Reduced Fat 2% Milk Singles are probably your best bet. Most tasters thought they tasted good or OK. I can tell you from a year of experience, they work well in a grilled cheese sandwich.

In the Monterey Jack cheese category, Sonoma Lite Jack cheeses were the definite favorite. The Garlic Jack was rated higher than the regular Monterey Jack, probably because it had more flavor; there was no noticeable difference between this garlic Jack and a regular-fat garlic Jack cheese. Even my pickiest tasters said they would buy this again. Most of the tasters thought

Taste vs. Fat

the regular Sonoma Lite Jack tasted good and said they would buy it again.

Kraft 1/3 Less Fat also tasted good in my opinion. Most of the tasters agreed. But there was one family that threw it away because they didn't like the taste or texture.

Making a low-fat ricotta cheese as opposed to a fat-free ricotta is probably as far as you can go and still have a good tasting ricotta with a similar texture to the original. The Precious Low Fat Ricotta does a nice job.

Not everyone is a Swiss cheese lover, but if you are, or if you make quiche or fondue occasionally, there are a few reduced-fat varieties available to you. Jarlsberg Lite is my favorite reduced-fat Swiss—it never disappoints me. Half of the tasters thought it tasted good and the others thought it tasted OK. Sargento makes a reduced-fat Swiss, and most of the tasters thought it tasted good; but there was one family that said they threw it away. Last in line is Alpine Lace's Reduced-Fat Swiss. The texture is real similar to regular Swiss, but it had a slight off flavor to me. Most tasters thought it tasted OK, but one family threw it away.

Fat-Free Cheese & Cheese Products

		Serving Size
★★	Healthy Choice Fat Free Pizza Cheese or Cheddar	1/4 cup (30g)
★★	Kraft Free American Singles	1 slice (21 g)
★	Kraft Healthy Favorites Fat Free Cheddar	1 oz
★	Precious Fat Free Mozzarella	1 oz
★	Precious Fat Free Ricotta	1/4 cup
★	Lifetime Fat Free Cheddar	1 oz

Key: 4 stars=great!, 3=good, 2=OK, 1=skip it

I am vehemently opposed to fat-free cheese. Cheese, by definition, is supposed to have some fat. Take all the fat out and, to me, you don't have "cheese" anymore. But if I had to buy a fat-free cheese, it would be the Healthy Choice line of grated fat-free cheese. It has a bland taste and an almost normal appearance. It worked better when accompanying highly flavored foods or when mixed with a good tasting reduced-fat cheese. A few tasters thought it tasted good; the rest thought it tasted OK if mixed with other foods.

Some of the tasters thought Kraft Free American Singles tasted good, some thought they tasted OK, and some threw them away. I thought they had an OK taste with a slight off-flavor. Then

Taste vs. Fat

Calories	Fat (g)	Saturated Fat (g)	Cholesterol (mg)	Sodium (mg)
45	0	0	<5	200
30	0	0	<5	300
50	0	0	<5	260
30	0	0	0.5	290
40	0	0	0	48
40	0	0	<5	220

comes the Kraft Healthy Favorites Fat Free Cheddar Cheese with a rather plastic appearance. I'm afraid it doesn't taste any better than it looks. The first bland taste is followed by a bad secondary taste. No one said they would buy this again. Precious Fat Free Mozzarella has slight mozzarella flavor but a bad aftertaste. Most of the tasters threw it out. Precious also makes a fat-free ricotta. It is very bland, which would be bad enough, but it also has a very undesirable texture in your mouth. Lifetime Fat Free Cheddar Cheese was horrible tasting—I couldn't even swallow it. Both the Precious Mozzarella and the Lifetime cheese looked very unappealing.

Cheese Puffs — Serving Size

★★★	Lite Cheddar Puffs 50% Less Fat	2 cups (30g)
★★	Planters Reduced Fat Cheez Balls	1 oz

Key: 4 stars=great!, 3=good, 2=OK, 1=skip it

The Lite Cheddar Puffs tasted very good—my kids loved them. They had a nice, simple flavor. I don't normally buy cheese puffs, but I might buy these again. Half the tasters agreed with me and thought the Lite Cheddar Puffs tasted good. The other half thought they tasted OK.

The Lite Cheddar Puffs get off to a good start with organic cornmeal listed as the first ingredient. What probably impressed me most was that they contain very few additives and

Canned Chili — Serving Size

★★★	Hormel Fat-Free Vegetarian Chili	1 cup

Key: 4 stars=great!, 3=good, 2=OK, 1=skip it

There are times when a can of chili in the cupboard can come in handy. According to the majority of tasters, that can may just as well be Hormel Fat-Free Vegetarian Chili. Most of the

Taste vs. Fat

Calories	Fat (g)	Saturated Fat (g)	Cholesterol (mg)	Sodium (mg)
(Little Bear Organic Foods, Carson, CA)				
150	5	1	5	280
140	6	1.5	<5	380

preservatives—a miracle, compared to other products in the cheese puff category. The only problem is you might have some trouble finding this specialty brand in your local grocery store.

Half the tasters thought the Planters Reduced Fat Cheez Balls tasted pretty good. The rest thought they tasted OK or said they threw them away because they didn't have any flavor. The best part about the Planters Cheez Balls is that you'll be able to find them in most supermarkets.

Calories	Fat (g)	Saturated Fat (g)	Cholesterol (mg)	Sodium (mg)
200	0	0	0	830

tasters thought it tasted good. The rest thought it tasted OK. The sodium is a little on the high side, so you definitely don't want to serve this chili with a salt shaker or with other high-sodium foods.

Chapter Six

Cinnamon Rolls		Serving Size
★★★	Entenmann's Reduced Fat Cinnamon Sweet Rolls	1 roll (61g)
★★★	Pillsbury Reduced Fat Cinnamon Rolls (in pop-type cans)	1 roll (44g)

Key: 4 stars=great!, 3=good, 2=OK, 1=skip it

The Pillsbury Reduced Fat Cinnamon Rolls are only slightly higher in fat (by weight) than the Entenmann's Cinnamon Sweet Rolls, while the Entenmann's are quite a bit higher in percentage of calories from sugar than the Pillsbury rolls. But which one tastes the best?

If you are sensitive to real sweet bakery items, you might prefer the Pillsbury cinnamon

Taste vs. Fat

Calories	Fat (g)	Saturated Fat (g)	Cholesterol (mg)	% Calories from sugar
190	5	1.5	35	40%
140	4	1	0	26%

rolls. But if you are sensitive to that ever-so-slight preservative flavor that tends to accompany the pop-type can products, you just might prefer the Entenmann's. Tasters found that they both tasted pretty good. You may need to warm the Entenmann's rolls in the microwave briefly though, to give them a softer, moister texture.

Chapter Six

Cold Cuts	Serving Size
Honey Ham:	
★★★★ Hillshire Farm Deli Select Honey Ham 97% Fat Free	3 slices (28g)
★★★1/2 Healthy Choice Deli Thin Sliced Honey Ham 97% Fat Free	3 slices (28g)
★★★ Oscar Mayer Honey Ham 96% Fat Free	1 1/2 slices (31g)
Bologna:	
★★★ Oscar Mayer Light Bologna	1 slice (28g)
★★★ Oscar Mayer Light Beef Bologna	1 slice (28g)
★ Oscar Mayer Fat Free Bologna	1 slice (28g)
Pepperoni:	
★★★★ Hormel Turkey Pepperoni 70% less fat	17 slices (30g)
Salami:	
★★★★ Gallo Light Italian Dry Salami	7 slices (28g)

Key: 4 stars=great!, 3=good, 2=OK, 1=skip it

Honey ham is honey ham is honey ham. Right? Not according to our tasters. Most of our tasters said they preferred Hillshire Farm Deli Select Honey Ham to the other choices. Hillshire Farm was described as tasting great by most of the tasters, while Healthy Choice Deli Thin and Oscar Mayer Honey Ham were described as good by half the tasters and great by the other half. But given those reviews, you can't go too wrong with Oscar

Taste vs. Fat

Calories	Fat (g)	Saturated Fat (g)	Cholesterol (mg)	Sodium (mg)
30	0.75	0.25	12	300
30	0.75	0.25	12	235
35	1.25	0.5	15	380
60	4	1.5	15	310
60	4	1.5	15	310
20	0	0	5	280
80	4	1.5	40	550
70	5	1.5	30	360

Mayer or Healthy Choice either.

The Oscar Mayer Honey Ham did have a tougher texture and thicker slices than the first two hams. All three hams contain sodium nitrite, but only Hillshire Farm's also contains vitamin C, which helps suppress the formation of the potentially carcinogenic nitrates from the nitrite it contains.

I don't think I've ever tasted bologna, and

Chapter Six

Cold Cuts (continued)

I'm not going to start now. But my tasters thought both of the Light Oscar Mayer bolognas tasted pretty good or OK. One family thought they tasted great. The tasters that normally buy bologna thought they might buy either of these bolognas again. As for the fat-free bologna, Oscar Mayer should have quit while it was ahead. The tasters thought it had a rubbery texture and no flavor. One family thought it tasted OK, but they would rather buy the light bologna.

Taste vs. Fat

The big winners in the cold cut category, though, are Hormel's Turkey Pepperoni and Gallo Light Salami. Everyone not only thought they tasted great, most liked them better than regular salami and pepperoni and said they would definitely look forward to buying them again. It doesn't get much better than this, folks!

Chapter Six

Fat-Free Cookies		Serving Size
Fruit Bars:		
★★★	Bakery Wagon Fat Free Strawberry Cobblers	1 (21g)
★★★	Fat Free Fig Newtons	2 (29g)
★★	Fat Free Peach Apricot Newtons Cobblers	1 (23g)
★★	Mother's Fat-Free Fig Bars	1 (21g)
★★	Strawberry Fat Free Newtons	2 (29g)
★	Keebler Delights Fruit Bars, Raspberry	1 (18g)
Chocolate:		
★★★1/2	SnackWell's Fat Free Chocolate Truffle	2 (36g)
★★	Pepperidge Farm Milk Chocolate Ripple	1 (18g)

Key: 4 stars=great!, 3=good, 2=OK, 1=skip it

My impression before writing this book was that I had never met a fat-free cookie I liked. And I have to say, after tasting every single one on the market, that view hasn't changed. But there were definitely other tasters who liked many of the fat-free cookies.

Of the fat-free fruit bars, most tasters thought the Bakery Wagon Fat Free Strawberry Cobbler tasted good and said they would buy it again. About half the tasters said they would buy the Fat Free Peach Apricot Newtons Cobblers

Taste vs. Fat

Calories	Fat (g)	Saturated Fat (g)	% Calories from sugar
70	0	0	57%
100	0	0	60%
60	0	0	53%
70	0	0	51%
100	0	0	64%
40	0	0	60%
120	0	0	53%
60	0	0	47%

again. But the rest of the tasters thought they tasted just OK or threw them away. The tasters who normally like fig bars thought the Fat Free Fig Newtons tasted good or OK. Most of the tasters thought Mother's Fat-Free Fig Bars tasted OK, and a few thought they tasted very good.

The Strawberry Fat Free Newtons tasted too sweet to me. I like a thicker cookie part, like you see in the cobbler selections in this list. Some tasters thought the Strawberry Newtons tasted good, but more said they tasted OK or threw them

Chapter Six

Fat-Free Cookies (continued)

out. Keebler Delights Raspberry Fruit Bars came in last because none of the tasters said they would buy them again. They didn't have a natural raspberry flavor. All of the tasters either thought they tasted OK or threw them away.

Now for the infamous (and expensive) fat-free chocolate cookies: SnackWell's makes several different variations on the fat-free chocolate cookie theme. We tasted the Chocolate Truffle Cookie; some people liked it and some people hated it. A little more than half the tasters said they were too sweet or had no flavor, and ended

Taste vs. Fat

up throwing them away. The rest of the tasters liked them, though, and said they would buy them again.

The Fat Free Milk Chocolate Ripple Pepperidge Farm cookie looks like it's going to taste fabulous. My taste buds were very disappointed after they got over the initial shock of sugar. These cookies are too sweet and they lack flavor. Most tasters thought they tasted bad but a there were a couple tasters that said they tasted good or OK. Only one family said they would buy them again.

Chapter Six

Low- & Reduced-Fat Cookies — Serving Size

Chocolate Chip:

★★★★	SnackWell's Reduced Fat Chocolate Chip (dough)	1/20th pkg.
★★★★	SnackWell's Reduced Fat Mini Chocolate Chip	13 (29g)
★★★	Reduced Fat Chips Ahoy	3 (32g)

Vanilla Sandwich Cookies:

★★★	Elfin Delights 50% Reduced Fat Vanilla	2 (25g)
★★★	SnackWell's Reduced Fat Creme	2 (26g)
★★1/2	Pepperidge Farm Reduced Fat Vanilla Creme Chantilly	2 (34g)
★★	Reduced Fat Vienna Fingers	2 (29g)

Chocolate Sandwich Cookies:

★★★	Reduced Fat Oreos	3 (32g)
★★★	Elfin Delights 50% Reduced Fat Chocolate	2 (25g)
★★	SnackWell's Reduced Fat Chocolate	2 (26g)
★★	Pepperidge Farm Reduced Fat Chocolate Creme Chantilly	2 (34g)
★★	Reduced Fat Hydrox	3 (31g)

Oatmeal:

★★★	Pepperidge Farms Reduced Fat Soft Baked Oatmeal Raisin	1 (26g)
★★	Bakery Wagon Lowfat Soft Oatmeal	1 (24g)

Key: 4 stars=great!, 3=good, 2=OK, 1=skip it

Taste vs. Fat

Calories	Fat (g)	Saturated Fat (g)	% Calories from sugar
110	4	1.5	40%
130	3.5	1.5	31%
150	6	1.5	27%
110	2.5	0.5	36%
110	2.5	0.5	36%
140	4	0	46%
130	3.5	0.5	31%
140	5	1	37%
110	2.5	0.5	29%
110	2.5	0.5	40%
140	4	0	40%
130	4	1	37%
110	3	0.5	36%
90	1.5	0	40%

Chapter Six

Low- & Reduced-Fat Cookies	Serving Size
Other:	
★★★★ Reduced Fat Deluxe Grahams	3 (26g)
★★★★ Healthy Choice Apricot/Raspberry Tart	2 (28g)
★★★ Reduced Fat Nilla Wafers	8 (29g)
★★ SnackWell's Chocolate Fudge Cookies (dough)	2
★★ Healthy Choice Fudge Creme	3 (33g)
★★ SnackWell's Golden Devil's Food	2 (32g)

Key: 4 stars=great!, 3=good, 2=OK, 1=skip it

Less-fat cookies—now we're talking! Many of the tasters were really happy with many of these cookies, but there was one family that didn't find any packaged chocolate chip cookies that they liked. So I gave them the SnackWell's chocolate chip cookie dough to try, and they liked it. It has a great flavor and texture if you like your chocolate chip cookies soft and chewy. If you don't, you will probably have good luck with SnackWell's Reduced Fat Mini Chocolate Chip Cookies (most tasters said they tasted good or great and would buy them again) or the Reduced Fat Chips Ahoy (most tasters thought they tasted good and would buy them again).

Elfin Delights Reduced Fat Vanilla Sandwich Cookies win that category by a hair. SnackWell's Reduced Fat Vanilla Sandwich

Taste vs. Fat

Calories	Fat (g)	Saturated Fat (g)	% Calories from sugar
120	5	2	37%
110	1.5	0	36%
120	2	0.5	40%
90	1.5	0	44%
130	2	1	52%
100	1	0	64%

Cookies also scored pretty high on taste. Most tasters thought both cookies tasted good or great and would buy them again. But there were a few tasters who thought the SnackWell's cookie tasted just OK. Pepperidge Farm just came out with a reduced-fat vanilla sandwich cookie of their own. It's a little fancier (and more expensive) than the others and it has a strong vanilla flavor. Most adult tasters thought it tasted good. My two young children didn't like it—probably because it looked a little too fancy for their taste. The majority of the tasters thought the Reduced Fat Vienna Fingers tasted OK—a little bland. A few tasters thought they tasted good.

Even though some tasters complained that the cookie part was a little tough, Reduced Fat Oreos surfaced as the best tasting chocolate

Chapter Six

Less-Fat Cookies (continued)

sandwich cookie, mainly because no one hated them. Almost half the tasters liked the first three chocolate sandwich cookies listed here, but the biggest difference between the three was whether or not any tasters hated them. Some tasters threw away the SnackWell's cookie, so that's what put them behind reduced-fat Oreo and Elfin Delights. Some tasters also commented that the Elfin Delights cookie was a bit bland. Most tasters were disappointed by Pepperidge Farm's Chocolate Creme Chantilly cookies. They looked so pretty and yet tasted just OK. In last place is the Reduced Fat Hydrox because only one family liked them and said they would buy them again. Everyone else thought they tasted OK. Some tasters commented on a strong, unfavorable malt flavor in the cookies.

Of the two reduced-fat oatmeal cookies available, one far exceeds the other in taste. The Pepperidge Farm Soft Baked Oatmeal Raisin has a good flavor and is just as it says—soft. Most tasters thought the other cookie, Bakery Wagon Lowfat Soft Oatmeal, tasted OK but needed more flavor. The texture was also nice and soft. The Pepperidge

Taste vs. Fat

Farm cookie has twice the fat of the Bakery Wagon, but less sugar. The difference in calories is 20 per cookie.

There were a couple other cookies I noticed and wanted to mention. The Reduced Fat Deluxe Grahams offer only a slight decrease in calories and fat from the regular version; 20 fewer calories and 2 fewer grams of fat per serving—with very little difference in flavor from the regular version. Healthy Choice very fancy Apricot and Raspberry Tart cookies are wonderful—most adults liked them. The Fudge Creme tart cookies, however, left a lot to be desired. Only one or two tasters liked these. You really had to look hard to find the fudge cream, which was probably just as well since it didn't have too much flavor anyway. The Reduced Fat Nilla Wafers can be used in recipes and as snacks with little noticeable difference in taste. SnackWell's Chocolate Fudge Cookie Dough tastes all right, not great. And the extra sweet SnackWell's Golden Devil's Food Cookies did not appeal to most tasters, although a couple people liked them.

Chapter Six

Crackers	Serving Size
Cheese Crackers:	
★★★★ SnackWell's Reduced Fat Zesty Cheese	32 (30g)
★★★1/2 Reduced Fat Cheese Nips	31 (30g)
★★★ Reduced Fat Cheez-It	30 (30g)
★★★ Wheatables Reduced Fat White Cheddar	27 (30g)
Club Crackers:	
★★★★ Keebler Reduced Fat Club	10 (32g)
Classic or Golden Crackers:	
★★★ Reduced Fat Hi-Ho	10 (30g)
★★★ Reduced Fat Ritz	10 (30g)
★★ Reduced Fat Town House	12 (30g)
★★ SnackWell's Classic Golden	12 (28g)
Graham Crackers:	
★★★★ Low Fat Honey Maid Cinnamon	8 (28g)
★ SnackWell's Cinnamon Graham Snacks	20 (30g)
Wheat Crackers:	
★★★★ SnackWell's Fat Free Wheat	10 (30g)
★★1/2 Reduced Fat Triscuit	8 (32g)
★★ Reduced Fat Wheat Thins	18 (29g)
Other Flavors:	
★★★1/2 SnackWell's Cracked Pepper	7 (15g)
★★★ Wheatables Reduced Fat Ranch	29 (30g)
★★ SnackWell's Reduced Fat French Onion	32 (30g)

Key: 4 stars=great!, 3=good, 2=OK, 1=skip it

Taste vs. Fat

Calories	Fat (g)	Saturated Fat (g)	Cholesterol (mg)	Sodium (mg)
120	2	0.5	<5	350
130	3.5	1	0	310
130	4.5	1	0	280
130	4	1	0	330
140	4	0	0	400
140	5	1	0	280
140	5	1	0	270
140	4	1	0	360
120	2	0	0	280
110	1.5	0	0	170
110	0	0	0	90
120	0	0	0	340
130	3	0.5	0	180
120	4	0.5	0	220
60	0	0	0	150
130	4	1	0	340
120	2	0	0	290

Chapter Six

Crackers (continued)

Tasters were, in general, very impressed with the reduced-fat and fat-free offerings in this supermarket aisle. For example, none of the cheese crackers listed here were really losers. Half the tasters liked all of them, for the most part, and said they would buy them again. Every taster thought the SnackWell's cracker tasted great and most of the tasters thought the Reduced Fat Cheese Nips tasted great or good. I couldn't notice any difference in taste or texture between these and the regular Cheese Nips (unless you count not feeling grease on my fingers). Half the tasters thought the Reduced Fat Cheez-Its tasted good; the rest thought they tasted OK. Half the tasters thought the Wheatables White Cheddar Crackers tasted good or great; the rest thought they tasted OK or threw them away. Some of the tasters complained that these last two crackers had a slight aftertaste.

There's only one selection in the club cracker category, and it wouldn't matter if there never was another selection, because the Keebler Reduced Fat Club Crackers do a perfect job. They taste great and they're nice and flaky like club crackers should be. Most of the tasters thought these tasted good or great and would buy them again. Only a few tasters rated them as OK.

The classic or golden cracker category has quite a few contestants but two brands outshone

Taste vs. Fat

the others. Reduced Fat Hi-Ho Crackers are nice and flaky and even have a buttery flavor. Most of the tasters rated these as good or great. Only a few tasters rated them as OK. Reduced Fat Ritz also taste good, with only a slight noticeable difference in flavor or texture from regular Ritz. Most of the tasters thought these tasted good and would buy these again. A couple tasters thought these tasted great and a couple thought they tasted OK.

There is a noticeable difference in taste between the Reduced Fat Town House crackers and the regular. Most of the tasters rated these as OK. Only a few tasters rated these as good or great. SnackWell's Classic Golden Crackers have an OK taste and texture, according to the majority of the tasters. Only one family rated them as good tasting and said they would buy them again.

Of the two low-fat graham cracker selections, the Lowfat Honey Maid Cinnamon Graham Crackers are definitely your best bet. They taste terrific with little difference in texture. The SnackWell's Cinnamon Graham Snacks have very little flavor and, frankly, only highly motivated adults seem to like them. Most of the tasters said they would not buy these again.

If a wheat cracker is what you're craving, you've got quite a few lower-fat options but only one that won the hearts of all the tasters. SnackWell's Fat Free Wheat Crackers tasted a lot

Chapter Six

Crackers (continued)

better than I remembered from a couple years ago. My guess is they reformulated because I remember something in the order of sawdust. These have a good, flaky texture, too. All the tasters rated them as great or good and all tasters said they would buy them again. Reactions were mixed to the Reduced Fat Triscuit. Most of the tasters rated them as good or OK. A couple rated them as great and a couple threw them away. I found it refreshing to find a cracker with only four ingredients in its ingredient list! The Reduced Fat Wheat Thins were only liked by a few tasters. Most

Cream Cheese	Serving Size
★★★1/2 Philadelphia Light	2 Tbsp.
★★ Philadelphia Free	2 Tbsp.

Key: 4 stars=great!, 3=good, 2=OK, 1=skip it

I use fat-free cream cheese all the time—as a fat replacement in cookie dough, biscuits and scones, and rich cakes. But what holds the place of honor on my bagel? Light cream cheese, of course. The tasters agreed. Most thought Philadelphia Light Cream Cheese tasted good or great and said they would definitely buy it again. A couple tasters thought it tasted OK. Half the tasters thought the fat-free version tasted OK and a couple tasters thought it tasted good, but the others threw it away, complaining of no flavor. The strange tex-

Taste vs. Fat

of the families thought they tasted OK but would not buy them again.

SnackWell's Cracked Pepper Crackers have a good flavor, particularly if you like pepper. Most of the tasters thought these crackers tasted great or good. Wheatables Reduced Fat Ranch Crackers were described as tasting good or great by two-thirds of the tasters. A third rated them as OK. SnackWell's Reduced Fat French Onion were liked by half the tasters. The rest thought they tasted OK or threw them away.

Calories	Fat (g)	Saturated Fat (g)	Cholesterol (mg)	Sodium (mg)
70	5	3.5	15	150
35	0	0	<5	180

ture didn't appeal to most of the tasters either.

Helpful Hint: Which cream cheese you should use to make a cheesecake really depends on how picky you are. You can make a pretty good cheesecake using half light and half fat-free cream cheese, adding grated lemon peel or some liqueur for flavor. If you are on the picky side, you can either use all light cream cheese or use half real cream cheese and half fat-free (it will have the same difference nutritionally).

Chapter Six

Crescent Rolls		Serving Size
★★★	Mrs. Wright's Crescent Dinner Rolls	2 rolls (56g)
★★★	Pillsbury Reduced Fat Crescent Rolls	2 rolls (56g)

Key: 4 stars=great!, 3=good, 2=OK, 1=skip it

Pigs in a blanket—aaah! A memory from my childhood. Piping hot hot dogs wrapped in crispy browned crescent roll dough fresh from the oven. Crescent roll dough comes in handy for quick dinner rolls or as an ingredient in many a recipe, courtesy of the Pillsbury Bake-Off contest. If you do need a can of crescent rolls, you may want to pass up the Pillsbury brand and reach for the store brand instead. I came across Mrs. Wright's cres-

Doughnuts		Serving Size
★★★	50% Less Fat Sara Lee Cinnamon Crumb Doughnuts	1
★★★	50% Less Fat Entenmann's Doughnuts	1

Key: 4 stars=great!, 3=good, 2=OK, 1=skip it

The tasters seemed to prefer the Sara Lee Cinnamon Crumb Doughnuts slightly over the Entenmann's. Two families thought the Sara Lee doughnuts tasted great, two thought they tasted good, and one family thought they tasted OK.

Taste vs. Fat

Calories	Fat (g)	Saturated Fat (g)	Cholesterol (mg)	Sodium (mg)
160	6	2	0	500
200	9	2	0	460

cent dinner rolls, which contained 40 fewer calories and 3 fewer grams of fat per 2-roll serving than Pillsbury's reduced-fat version.

Pillsbury's reduced-fat crescent rolls tasted good to most of my tasting families. I thought they had more of a bread texture and less of a flaky, pastry texture, though, compared to Mrs. Wright's.

Calories	Fat (g)	Saturated Fat (g)	Cholesterol (mg)	% Calories from sugar
200	7	2	5	18%
180	6	1.5	15	33%

Most of the families thought the Entenmann's doughnuts tasted good and the rest thought they tasted OK. Both doughnuts are less greasy than regular doughnuts and can be frozen, then thawed in the microwave when needed.

Chapter Six

Egg Substitutes	Serving Size
★★★ Egg Beaters (Nabisco)	1/4 cup
★★ Second Nature	1/4 cup
★ Scramblers (Morningstar Farms)	1/4 cup

Key: 4 stars=great!, 3=good, 2=OK, 1=skip it

The oldest fat-free egg substitute is still the best—Egg Beaters. A little more than half of the tasters thought it tasted great and would buy it again. Two families threw it away, one without even tasting it. Of the three substitutes, Egg Beaters looks the most like real scrambled eggs. One family thought Second Nature Egg Substitutes tasted good, and another family thought it tasted OK, but the rest of the tasters threw it away. One family thought

Taste vs. Fat

Calories	Fat (g)	Saturated Fat (g)	Cholesterol (mg)	Sodium (mg)
30	0	0	0	100
40	0	0	0	115
35	0	0	0	95

Scramblers Egg Substitute tasted OK. The rest of the tasters threw it away. Both Second Nature and Scramblers have an unnatural appearance.

Helpful Hint: When making scrambled eggs, quiche, or omelettes, I use half real eggs and half Egg Beaters egg substitute. This mixture is very similar to real eggs but with half the fat, saturated fat, and cholesterol.

Chapter Six

Frosting		Serving Size
★★★	SnackWell's Chocolate Fudge Frosting	2 Tbsp
★★★	Reduced Fat Sweet Rewards Vanilla	2 Tbsp
★★	Betty Crocker Low-Fat Vanilla	2 Tbsp

Key: 4 stars=great!, 3=good, 2=OK, 1=skip it

Sweet Rewards has two grams more fat per serving (2 tablespoons) than their low-fat vanilla option, but boy do those two grams make a difference. The Sweet Rewards frosting had a much better flavor than the low-fat frosting, which just tasted OK. If you buy the low-fat frosting and decide you don't much like the flavor, blend it with a regular-fat frosting of your choice.

Taste vs. Fat

Calories	Fat (g)	Saturated Fat (g)	Cholesterol (mg)	% Calories from sugar
120	3	1	0	67%
130	2.5	1	0	74%
120	0.5	0.5	0	80%

Better yet, try the new SnackWell's Chocolate Fudge frosting. This frosting seemed creamier and not quite as sweet, probably because it has a little more fat per serving and the lowest percentage of calories from sugar of all three.

Chapter Six

Frozen Entrées		Serving Size
Lasagna:		
★★	Healthy Choice Lasagna Roma with Meat Sauce	1
★★	Weight Watchers Lasagna with Meat Sauce	1
Fettuccini Alfredo:		
★★★	Healthy Choice Chicken Fettucine Alfredo	1
★★★	Lean Cuisine Chicken Fettuccini	1
★★	Weight Watchers Fettuccini with Broccoli	1
Chicken with Rice:		
★★★	Lean Cuisine Chicken Piccata	1
★★★	Healthy Choice Garlic Chicken Milano	1
★1/2	The Budget Gourmet Light Rice and Chicken with Mozzarella in Zesty Tomato Sauce	1
French Bread Pizza:		
★★	Healthy Choice Cheese French Bread Pizza	1
★★	Lean Cuisine French Bread Pizza, Pepperoni	1
Meatloaf or Salisbury Steak:		
★★★	Weight Watchers Salisbury Steak	1
★★	Healthy Choice Salisbury Steak	1
★	Lean Cuisine Meatloaf	1

Key: 4 stars=great!, 3=good, 2=OK, 1=skip it

Taste vs. Fat

Calories	Fat (g)	Saturated Fat (g)	Cholesterol (mg)	Sodium (mg)
390	5	2	15	580
270	7	3	35	570
260	4.5	2	40	410
270	6	2.5	45	580
230	6	3	20	450
290	6	1.5	30	540
240	4	2	35	510
270	6	2	25	400
310	4	2	10	470
330	7	3	25	590
250	9	3.5	40	590
260	6	2.5	30	500
250	7	2	45	570

Chapter Six

Frozen Entrées (continued)

I am not a frozen entrée person, but I know that many people rely on them for meals at work and home. Of the two lasagna choices, Healthy Choice seemed to fair a little better than Weight Watchers. A third of the tasters thought it tasted good, and two-thirds thought it tasted OK. I found myself adding a tablespoon of freshly grated Parmesan cheese to both lasagnas. The Healthy Choice lasagna had a more realistic serving size, too. Tasters thought the Weight Watchers tasted just OK.

Healthy Choice Chicken Fettucini Alfredo is, according to the tasters, the best tasting of the fettucini alfredo entrées. Half the tasters thought it tasted great or good and the other half thought it tasted OK. I found the sauce watery and had to add freshly grated Parmesan cheese to it. I liked the Lean Cuisine Chicken Fettucini the best. The taste and texture were both appealing. The chicken was tender and good tasting. Half the tasters agreed with me; the others thought it was OK. Nobody thought the Weight Watchers Fettucini with Broccoli tasted any better than OK.

The Lean Cuisine Chicken Piccata and the Healthy Choice Garlic Chicken Milano tied in the chicken and rice category. A third of the tasters thought both tasted great, a third thought they tasted good, and a third thought they tasted OK or threw it away. I personally liked the Chicken

Taste vs. Fat

Piccata better. I'm not even sure the Budget Gourmet Light Rice and Chicken with Mozzarella in Zesty Tomato Sauce belongs in the chicken and rice category. I counted only three bite-size pieces of chicken. Half the tasters thought it tasted OK and half threw it out.

Both of the French bread pizzas were rated OK by most of the tasters—no one was too excited about them. The Healthy Choice came out looking only a little better than the Lean Cuisine because one family thought it tasted good. The Healthy Choice pizza was pretty skimpy on the cheese, but what do you expect for 4 grams of fat. I broiled it briefly to bubble the cheese on top.

The winner in the meatloaf/Salisbury steak category was basically the brand that had the fewest number of tasters throwing it away—that would be Weight Watchers Salisbury Steak. Half the tasters thought it tasted good or great; the rest thought it tasted OK. I found it mind-boggling to find 60 ingredients for something as seemingly simple as Salisbury steak and potatoes. Half the tasters thought the Healthy Choice Salisbury Steak tasted good or OK. The rest threw it away. The majority of the tasters threw the Lean Cuisine Meatloaf away. One family thought it tasted OK. The only nice thing I can say about this entrée is that the mashed potatoes tasted good.

Chapter Six

Granola Bars	Serving Size
Chocolate Dipped:	
★★★ SnackWell's Fudge Dipped Granola Bars, Original	1 bar (28g)
Chewy:	
★★1/2 Nature Valley Low Fat Chewy Variety Pack	1 bar (28g)
★★1/2 Quaker Chewy Lowfat Granola Bars, Oatmeal Cookie	1 bar (28g)
★ Health Valley Fat-Free Granola Bars, Chocolate Chip	1 bar (42g)
Crunchy:	
★★★ Nature Valley Reduced Fat Crunchy Granola Bars, Oats 'n Honey	1 bar (23g)

Key: 4 stars=great!, 3=good, 2=OK, 1=skip it

There is only one reduced-fat alternative in the "fudge-dipped" granola bar category: SnackWell's Fudge Dipped Granola Bar. This bar would be hard to beat unless you were taste testing it side by side with a chocolate covered Kudos bar —which, by the way, tastes better. The small sized SnackWell's bar, though, would be best described as "skinny" dipped—because if you sneeze you might miss the chocolate coating! But frankly, this is probably just enough chocolate flavor for most people, and besides, what do you expect from 1.5 grams of fat!

In the chewy category, Nature Valley Chewy Granola Bars led the pack by only a mar-

Taste vs. Fat

Calories	Fat (g)	Saturated Fat (g)	Cholesterol (mg)	% Calories from sugar
110	1.5	1.5	0	51%
110	2	0	0	25%
110	2	0.5	0	36%
140	0	0	0	40%
100	3	0	0	28%

gin. Half the tasters thought they tasted good and the others thought they tasted OK. Half the tasters also thought the Quaker Chewy Granola Bars tasted good. The rest thought they tasted OK, except for one taster who threw them away because they tasted too sweet. Health Valley Fat Free Chocolate Chip Granola Bars tasted just plain bad—I had to spit my first bite out, it was so bad. All the tasters threw them out except for a couple of tasters who thought it tasted OK. As for crunchy granola bars, Nature Valley's Oats 'n Honey rated quite well. Two families thought it tasted great. The rest thought they tasted good or OK.

Chapter Six

Hot Dogs and Franks		Serving Size
★★★★	Ball Park Lite Franks	1 (57g)
★★★★	Louis Rich Turkey Franks	1 (57g)
★★★	Healthy Choice Deli Style Low Fat Beef Franks	1 (75g)
★★★	Healthy Choice Low Fat Jumbo Franks	1 (57g)
	Hormel Light & Lean 97	1 (45g)
★1/2	Butterball Fat Free Franks	1 (45g)
★1/2	Oscar Mayer Free Hot Dogs	1 (50g)
★1/2	Ball Park Fat Free Franks	1 (50g)

Key: 4 stars=great!, 3=good, 2=OK, 1=skip it

One of my families couldn't even bring themselves to taste the hot dogs with only half the fat removed. I guess to them a hot dog is a hot dog, and it shouldn't be messed with—certainly not by turkeys. I, on the other hand, welcomed the 50 percent less fat hot dogs with open arms. There are only two reduced-fat franks my husband likes, and they happen to be the top rated ones here. Both Ball Park Lite and Louis Rich Turkey Franks were described as having a good texture and tast-

Taste vs. Fat

Calories	Fat (g)	Saturated Fat (g)	Cholesterol (mg)	Sodium (mg)
110	8	2	20	730
110	8	2.5	50	630
100	3	1	35	480
70	1.5	0.5	30	530
45	1	0.5	15	490
45	0	0	15	480
40	0	0	15	490
40	0	0	15	560

ing great and good by the tasters. Tasters thought the Healthy Choice Deli Style Low Fat Beef Franks and Low Fat Jumbo Franks tasted good and OK. And here's where the better reviews stop. Once you get down to 1 gram of fat per frank (or less) you will notice a taste and texture that leaves a lot to be desired. The Hormel Light & Lean and the fat-free franks tasted good and OK to less than half the tasters. The rest threw them away.

Chapter Six

Light Ice Cream	Serving Size
Vanilla and Vanilla Based:	
★★★★ Breyer's Light Vanilla	1/2 cup
★★1/2 Dreyer's Grand Light Vanilla	1/2 cup
★★1/2 SnackWell's Brownie Sundae	1/2 cup
★★ Healthy Choice Fudge Brownie à la Mode	1/2 cup
Chocolate:	
★★★★ Dreyer's Grand Light Rocky Road	1/2 cup
★★★★ Healthy Choice Special Creations Turtle Fudge Cake	1/2 cup
★★★ Mattus' Lowfat Chocolate Chocolate Cookie	1/2 cup
★★ Breyer's Light Rocky Road	1/2 cup
Coffee:	
★★★★ Dreyer's Grand Light Espresso Fudge Chip	1/2 cup
★★★★ Healthy Choice Special Creations Cappuccino Mocha Fudge	1/2 cup
★★★★ Baskin Robbins 31-Lowfat Espresso 'n Cream	1/2 cup
★★ Healthy Choice Cappuccino Chocolate Chunk	1/2 cup
Cherry:	
★★★ Healthy Choice Special Creations Cherry Chocolate Chunk	1/2 cup

Key: 4 stars=great!, 3=good, 2=OK, 1=skip it

Taste vs. Fat

Calories	Fat (g)	Saturated Fat (g)	Cholesterol (mg)	% Calories from sugar
130	4.5	3	35	46%
100	4	2.5	25	44%
130	2	1	5	61%
120	2	1	5	50%
110	4	2	20	44%
130	2	1	<5	71%
170	3	2	10	66%
120	2	1	0	23%
110	4	2.5	15	51%
120	2	1	<5	63%
110	2.5	1	5	58%
120	2	1	10	47%
110	2	1	<5	69%

Chapter Six

Light Ice Cream (continued)

I thought I would never see the end to all the ice cream cartons in my freezer. But it was worth it—we found a handful of great tasting lower-fat ice creams that most everyone loved. Everyone liked Breyer's Light Vanilla. They thought it either tasted great or good. Dreyer's Grand Light was rated as tasting good or OK. But some tasters wanted to throw it out because of its noncreamy texture and taste. SnackWell's Brownie Sundae wasn't very creamy but half the tasters thought it tasted pretty good. The other half thought it tasted OK. Healthy Choice Fudge Brownie à la Mode has a slight odd taste. Most tasters thought it tasted OK.

Breyer's and Dreyer's switch places in the chocolate ice cream category. What Dreyer's lost in light vanilla ice cream, it gained in the chocolate category. The two top winners in the chocolate category are Dreyer's Grand Light Rocky Road and Healthy Choice Special Creations Turtle

Taste vs. Fat

Fudge Cake. All the tasters, with the exception of one or two, thought these tasted great! Mattus' Lowfat Chocolate Chocolate Cookie was rated as tasting good or great by most tasters. A couple rated it as OK because they thought it tasted too sweet. Breyer's is last in this list because most of the tasters thought its Rocky Road tasted OK. A few tasters thought it tasted good.

It's a three-way tie in the coffee ice cream category. Tasters thought all three—Dreyer's Grand Light Espresso Fudge Chip, Healthy Choice Special Creations Cappuccino Mocha Fudge, and Baskin Robbins Espresso 'n Cream—tasted good or great and they would buy them again. They left Healthy Choice Cappuccino Chocolate Chunk in the dust because almost every taster said they wouldn't buy this again, rating the taste as just OK.

Standing proud is Healthy Choice Special Creations Cherry Chocolate Chunk—the only light cherry flavor in the light ice cream category. Everyone who tasted this ice cream thought it tasted good. I thought it tasted great.

Chapter Six

Fat-Free Frozen Yogurt & Ice Cream		Serving Size
★★1/2	Breyers Free Vanilla Fudge Twirl	1/2 cup
★★	Häagen-Dazs Fat Free, Vanilla	1/2 cup
★★	Dannon Light Fat Free, Lemon Chiffon	1/2 cup
★	Dreyer's Fat Free Chocolate Fudge	1/2 cup
★	Dreyer's Fat Free Vanilla Chocolate Swirl	1/2 cup

Key: 4 stars=great!, 3=good, 2=OK, 1=skip it

If Häagen-Dazs can't make a fat-free ice cream that everyone likes, who can? A few tasters thought their Fat Free Vanilla Frozen Yogurt tasted pretty good, considering it was fat free. But the rest of the tasters thought it was OK or bad tasting. The top rated brand, though, is Breyer's Free Vanilla Fudge Twirl, which tasted good or OK to the majority of tasters. Almost every taster

Taste vs. Fat

Calories	Fat (g)	Saturated Fat (g)	Cholesterol (mg)	% Calories from sugar
110	0	0	0	55%
140	0	0	<5	49%
90	0	0	0	22%
110	0	0	0	51%
90	0	0	0	58%

thought Dannon's Light Fat Free Frozen Yogurt Lemon Chiffon tasted at least OK, and some said it was good. But half the tasters noticed a bothersome aftertaste (it is sweetened with NutraSweet). Dreyer's Fat Free Chocolate Fudge and Fat Free Vanilla Chocolate Swirl battled it out for last place. Most tasters said they would throw them away. Only one taster thought they tasted good.

Chapter Six

Low-Fat Frozen Yogurt		Serving Size
★★★1/2	Ben & Jerry's Low Fat Cherry Garcia	1/2 cup
★★1/2	Ben & Jerry's Chocolate Fudge Brownie Low Fat	1/2 cup
★★1/2	Ben & Jerry's Chocolate Chip Cookie Dough	1/2 cup
★	Dreyer's Low Fat Vanilla Frozen Yogurt	1/2 cup

Key: 4 stars=great!, 3=good, 2=OK, 1=skip it

Ben & Jerry's regular Cherry Garcia is my best friend's favorite ice cream ever. So it was with skepticism that I asked her to try the low-fat frozen yogurt version. I don't know if she was more surprised or if I was, but she liked it! She said she couldn't taste the difference between the low-fat and the regular. Ben & Jerry, you've done it again. Everyone who tasted it thought it was good or great tasting. Was it my imagination,

Taste vs. Fat

Calories	Fat (g)	Saturated Fat (g)	Cholesterol (mg)	% Calories from sugar
170	3	2	10	71%
190	3	1.5	5	72%
210	3.5	2.5	10	57%
100	2.5	1.5	10	56%

though, or does the low-fat version have way fewer chocolate chunks? Oh well. The next two selections, Ben & Jerry's Chocolate Fudge Brownie and Chocolate Chip Cookie Dough, were rated exactly the same. Half the tasters thought they tasted good and half thought they tasted OK. Most of the tasters wanted to throw away Dreyer's Low Fat Vanilla Frozen Yogurt. Just a few tasters thought it tasted OK.

Chapter Six

Ice Cream Bars	Serving Size
★★★★ Milky Way Reduced Fat Vanilla Ice Cream Bars	1 bar (48g)
★★★★ Klondike Reduced Fat No Sugar Added Vanilla Ice Cream with Chocolate Coating	1 bar (113g)
★★★ SnackWell's Low-Fat Ice Cream Sandwich	1 sandwich (45g)
★★★ Betty Crocker Healthy Temptations Snack Sandwiches	1 sandwich (36g)
★ Klondike Fat Free Big Bear Ice Cream Sandwich	1 sandwich (118mg)

Key: 4 stars=great!, 3=good, 2=OK, 1=skip it

The first two selections are still a bit high in calories and fat for my liking—but apparently the original versions are much higher than these are. They both taste like the real thing to me. Milky Way's Reduced Fat Vanilla Ice Cream Bars are very satisfying; everyone loved them. And Klondike's Reduced Fat No Sugar Added Vanilla Bars taste terrific too. A couple of tasters did notice that NutraSweet aftertaste (although I didn't). It does contain 6 grams of natural sugar per serving and 4 grams of sugar alcohols per serving (which can cause diarrhea in some people when consumed in

Taste vs. Fat

Calories	Fat (g)	Saturated Fat (g)	Cholesterol (mg)	% Calories from sugar
140	7	3	5	48.5%
190	10	7	5	13%
100	1.5	1	5	40%
80	1.5	0.5	<5	35%
150	0	0	0	40%

larger amounts). The Betty Crocker Healthy Temptations Snack Sandwiches taste pretty good. The cookie part is a little on the crunchy side— but heck, for 1 1/2 grams of fat, beggars can't be choosers. The SnackWell's low-fat ice cream sandwiches fared a little better with tasters, probably because the cookie part was tender. The ice cream filling, however, was ice milk-like. In last place were Klondike Fat Free Big Bear ice cream sandwiches, which were described as "yucky" by most tasters. The ice cream part was "bear"able, but the cookie part was tough and had an odd taste.

Chapter Six

Ice Cream Toppings		Serving Size
★★1/2	Mrs. Richardson's Fat Free Hot Fudge	2 Tbsp.
★★1/2	Mrs. Richardson's Fat Free Caramel Sauce	2 Tbsp.
★★	Smucker's Light Toppings Fat Free Hot Fudge	2 Tbsp.
★	Smucker's Fat Free Caramel Topping	2 Tbsp.

Key: 4 stars=great!, 3=good, 2=OK, 1=skip it

No one said they would throw Mrs. Richardson's Fat Free Hot Fudge away. That's a good start. Most everyone thought this tasted as least OK; some said it tasted good and one taster thought it was excellent. It has a nice thick texture. A couple of families actually liked Mrs. Richardson's Fat Free Caramel Sauce, and a couple thought it tasted just OK. Some tasters, on the other hand, wanted to throw away Smucker's Fat Free Hot Fudge. It has a strong cocoa flavor. Only one taster thought it tasted good. The Smucker's has an added bonus—a serving contains 2 grams of fiber, which comes from the cellulose gel and other undigestable starches that are used as thickeners.

Taste vs. Fat

Calories	Fat (g)	Saturated Fat (g)	Cholesterol (mg)	% Calories from sugar
110	0	0	0	65%
130	0	0	0	62%
90	0	0	0	67%
130	0	0	0	65%

Almost everyone said they would throw away Smucker's Fat Free Caramel Topping. It has a thin consistency compared to regular caramel sauce. I would rather use half as much regular caramel sauce, which contains 65 calories and 0.75 grams of fat per tablespoon; obviously, the tasters agreed with me.

Helpful Hint: If you want a hot fudge topping that is not fat free but is still lower in fat than most, try the Hot Fudge Microwave Topping by Smucker's. A 2-tablespoon serving contains 130 calories and 2.5 grams of fat. And the best part is, it tastes like real hot fudge.

Chapter Six

	Diet Margarine & Light Butter	Serving Size
★★★	I Can't Believe It's Not Butter Light	1 Tbsp.
★★	Land O Lakes Light Butter	1 Tbsp.
★★	Parkay 1/3 Less Fat Spread	1 Tbsp.
★★	Fleischmann's Lower Fat Margarine	1 Tbsp.
★★	Imperial Light Margarine	1 Tbsp.
★	Weight Watchers Light Margarine	1 Tbsp.
★	Smart Beat Lower Fat Margarine	1 Tbsp.

Key: 4 stars=great!, 3=good, 2=OK, 1=skip it

Some tasters took this assignment better than others. Apparently choosing a butter or margarine is a very personal thing. Those of us that were raised on cheap margarine may be more open minded; then again maybe some of us have rebelled against our youth and are now religious about using only butter. It's hard to say why we all have the attitudes and tolerances we have when it comes to tasting diet margarines. I'll tell you one thing's for sure, some people are way more accepting in this category than others. You might wonder why the fat-free margarines weren't part of the tasting. Because that's where this Registered Dietitian draws the line. I am unilaterally opposed to fat-free versions of foods that naturally have a lot of fat. Besides, I had my work cut out for me just in

Taste vs. Fat

Calories	Fat (g)	Saturated Fat (g)	Cholesterol (mg)	Sodium (mg)
50	6	1	0	90
50	6	4	20	70
70	7	1.5	0	120
40	4.5	0	0	90
50	6	1	0	140
45	4	1	0	70
20	2	0	0	105

the diet margarine category.

I Can't Believe It's Not Butter Light was liked by most of the tasters. Three families now use this product because they thought it was the best tasting margarine (I've been using this for years now). Most tasters thought Land O Lakes Light Butter tasted OK. One family thought it tasted good. A third of the tasters thought Parkay 1/3 Less Fat Spread was good, a third thought it was OK, and a third threw it away because it didn't have any flavor. Most tasters thought Fleischmann's Lower Fat Margarine and Imperial Light were OK; the rest wanted to throw them away. Most of the tasters that tried the Weight Watchers and Smart Beat margarines wanted to throw them away.

Chapter Six

Mayonnaise		Serving Size
★★★★	Best Foods regular mayo blended with nonfat sour cream	1 Tbsp
★★★	Best Foods Light	1 Tbsp
★★★	Best Foods Low Fat	1 Tbsp
★★	Miracle Whip Light	1 Tbsp
★	Kraft Light	1 Tbsp
★	Kraft Free Nonfat	1 Tbsp
★	Miracle Whip Free	1 Tbsp
★	Weight Watchers Fat Free	1 Tbsp

Key: 4 stars=great!, 3=good, 2=OK, 1=skip it

Most everyone that tasted the different types of mayonnaise agreed on three things—number one: Fat-free mayo is best left on the shelf. Only the super health-motivated tasters thought is was acceptable, but still not great. Number two: The light mayos with half the fat of regular mayonnaise tasted OK. People who grew up on Miracle Whip tended to prefer the Light Miracle Whip, whereas people who grew up on Best Foods mayo preferred the Best Foods Light mayo. Some would buy it again and some would not. Number three: The next best thing to the real thing might just be using less of the real thing. I tried blending real mayonnaise with my favorite nonfat sour cream. Everyone loved it. If making a potato, macaroni, or shrimp salad, you can use one-third real mayo,

Taste vs. Fat

Calories	Fat (g)	Saturated Fat (g)	Cholesterol (mg)	Sodium (mg)
55	5.5	2.3	2.5	46
50	5	1	5	115
25	1	0	0	140
40	3	n/a	0	120
50	5	1	5	90
10	0	0	0	105
15	0	0	0	105
10	0	0	0	105

one-third low-fat mayo, and one-third nonfat sour cream, or two-thirds nonfat sour cream and one-third real mayo. These homemade alternatives seem to go over much better with people who really love the real thing or are sensitive to the undesirable tastes and aftertastes in the reduced-fat or no-fat versions.

Best Foods Light works well on a sandwich or mixed in with something. One family couldn't tell the difference between this and regular mayo. Two families said it tasted good and great, and although they could taste the difference, they would still buy it again. Half the tasters thought Best Foods Low Fat tasted good or great. The other half thought it tasted just OK. While some of the tasters thought Miracle Whip Light

Mayonnaise (continued)

tasted good or OK, others said they would throw it out.

From the Kraft Light Mayonnaise on down to Weight Watcher's Fat Free Mayonnaise—most of the tasters said they would throw these brands out. Comments ranged from "yucky" and "bad eggy taste and smell," to "made my tongue numb" and "strange aftertaste."

Muffin Mixes	Serving Size
Blueberry:	
★★★ Betty Crocker Fat Free Wild Blueberry Muffin Mix	1/12th mix
★★★ Krusteaz Fat Free Wild Blueberry Muffin Mix	1/10th mix
Apple:	
★★ Betty Crocker Fat Free Apple Cinnamon Muffin Mix	1/12 mix

Key: 4 stars=great!, 3=good, 2=OK, 1=skip it

Both Betty Crocker's Fat Free Wild Blueberry Muffin Mix and Krusteaz Fat Free Wild Blueberry Muffin Mix taste good, but Betty Crocker's muffins have Krusteaz beat in texture. Krusteaz

Taste vs. Fat

Helpful Hint: Since the best tasting light mayonnaise is still a little too high in fat (for my liking) when used to make dressings, pasta, or potato salads, I like to blend Best Foods Light with Best Foods Low Fat (1 to 1 ratio) to make a good tasting mayonnaise with 3 grams of fat per tablespoon. If you are going to use the low-fat or fat-free mayonnaise straight from the jar for your dressing, pasta, or potato salads, zip up the flavor by adding dill pickle juice, Dijon mustard, etc.

Calories	Fat (g)	Saturated Fat (g)	Sodium (mg)	% Calories from sugar
120	0	0	190	50%
143	0	0	330	43%
110	0	0	180	47%

muffins are a bit crumbly. Most of the tasters thought Betty Crocker Fat Free Apple Cinnamon Muffins tasted OK, and a few said they would buy it again.

Chapter Six

Pancake & Waffle Mixes		Serving Size
★★★	Reduced Fat Bisquick	1/3 cup mix
★★★	Krusteaz Lite Oat Bran	1/2 cup mix
★★	Mrs. Butterworth's Low Fat Buttermilk Complete	1/3 cup mix
★★	Krusteaz Fat Free Buttermilk	1/2 cup mix

Key: 4 stars=great!, 3=good, 2=OK, 1=skip it

Reduced Fat Bisquick is a staple in my house. We use it to make quick pancakes, waffles, and biscuits. I like to use low-fat buttermilk in place of half the skim milk called for, though, to add a little texture and flavor. Half the tasters thought it tasted good and half thought it tasted OK. Many of the tasters thought the Krusteaz Lite Oat Bran Pancake Mix had a good flavor. It can get a little gummy in the middle of the pancake, though. I prefer to use 1/2 cup low-fat buttermilk and a cup

Taste vs. Fat

Calories	Fat (g)	Saturated Fat (g)	Cholesterol (mg)	Sodium (mg)
150	2.5	0.5	0	460
140	1	0	0	390
150	2	0.5	10	630
190	0	0	0	440

or so of water in place of the 1 1/2 cups water called for on the box.

Most tasters thought Mrs. Butterworth's Low Fat Buttermilk Complete tasted OK. It tasted a little better to me when I added low-fat buttermilk in place of some of the water called for. It was difficult to get the right consistency with the Krusteaz Fat Free Buttermilk Pancake Mix. But even if you do, it still will taste bland.

Chapter Six

Peanut Butter		Serving Size
★★★	Reduced Fat Jif	2 Tbsp.
★★★	Laura Scudder's Reduced Fat	2 Tbsp.
★★	Reduced Fat Skippy	2 Tbsp.

Key: 4 stars=great!, 3=good, 2=OK, 1=skip it

Peanut butter lovers now have a good tasting reduced-fat option—Jif! Most of the tasters thought it tasted good or great. One of our tasters even liked it better than regular peanut butter (I wouldn't go quite that far). If you like the thick, natural style peanut butter, you will probably prefer Laura Scudder's new reduced-fat version.

Microwave Popcorn		Serving Size
★★★	Orville Redenbacher's Light Butter	6 cups
★★★	Newman's Own Light Butter Flavor	3.5 cups
★★★	Pop Secret Light Butter	6 cups
★★★	Healthy Choice Lowfat Butter Flavor	3 Tbsp. (unpopped)

Key: 4 stars=great!, 3=good, 2=OK, 1=skip it

There aren't big differences between the brands in this category. Half the tasters liked them all about the same (great or good) and about half said they

Taste vs. Fat

Calories	Fat (g)	Saturated Fat (g)	Cholesterol (mg)	Sodium (mg)
190	12	2.5	0	250
200	12	2	0	120
180	12	2.5	0	170

Although tasters preferred the Jif, they thought Laura Scudder's peanut butter tasted pretty good. Most of the tasters thought reduced-fat Skippy tasted good or OK. I was raised on Skippy so it is with great sadness that I tell you the taste was flatter than Jif's.

Calories	Fat (g)	Saturated Fat (g)	Cholesterol (mg)	Sodium (mg)
120	3	1	0	360
110	3	1	0	90
140	6	1	0	250
130	2.5	0	0	340

wouldn't buy them again because they would rather make homemade popcorn.

Chapter Six

Pop-Tarts and Breakfast/Snack Bars		Serving Size
★★★	Kellogg's Low Fat Pop-Tarts, Strawberry	1 (52g)
★★★	SnackWell's Toaster Pastries, Iced Strawberry	1 (48g)
★★1/2	SnackWell's Cereal Bars, Strawberry	1 (37g)
★★1/2	Nutri-Grain Cereal Bars, Raspberry	1 (37g)
★	Sweet Rewards Snack Bars, Strawberry	1 (37g)

Key: 4 stars=great!, 3=good, 2=OK, 1=skip it

The majority of tasters were quite happy with the new low-fat Pop-Tarts by Kellogg's. Two families thought they tasted OK. Not to be outdone, SnackWell's came out with their own toaster pastries, which are even lower in fat. They are less of a pastry than the Kellogg's Pop-Tarts, but they have a similar taste. Half the tasters liked SnackWell's cereal bars, the other half thought they tasted OK. I thought they were too sweet. I liked the Nutri-

Taste vs. Fat

Calories	Fat (g)	Saturated Fat (g)	% Calories from Sugar	Fiber (mg)
190	3	0.5	40%	1
170	1	0	49%	1
120	0	0	53%	1
140	3	0.5	34%	1
120	0	0	60%	—

Grain cereal bars myself, because they weren't as sweet as the others. About a third of the tasters thought they tasted good, a third thought they tasted OK, and a third threw them away. Most of the tasters threw the Sweet Rewards bars away. They were way too sweet for me, which is not surprising considering they have the highest percentage of calories from sugar of the whole lot.

Chapter Six

Potato Chips		Serving Size
★★★	Reduced Fat Lay's	1 oz
★★★	Pringles Right Crisps	1 oz
★★1/2	Reduced Fat Ruffles	1 oz
★★1/2	Baked Lay's Barbecue Potato Crisps	1 oz
★★1/2	Baked Lay's Potato Crisps	1 oz
★★	Mother's Potato Snaps	1 oz

Key: 4 stars=great!, 3=good, 2=OK, 1=skip it

Every now and then a good potato chip (or two) really hits the spot. So, if I can find some lower-fat potato chips that taste pretty much the same as regular potato chips, then why not buy them? I was pretty happy with Pringles Right Crisps and Reduced Fat Ruffles, but my heart now belongs to Reduced Fat Lay's. I know manufacturers can take a little fat out and still have a good tasting potato chip, but can they take all the fat out? They can and they did—but it sure doesn't taste the same. Fat-free potato chips came up many times in my survey of products people tried and hated.

    Half the tasters thought Reduced Fat Lay's and Pringles Right Crisps tasted good or great. The rest thought they tasted OK or threw them

Taste vs. Fat

Calories	Fat (g)	Saturated Fat (g)	Cholesterol (mg)	Sodium (mg)
140	6.7	1	0	30
140	7	2	0	135
140	6.7	1	0	130
110	1.5	0	0	220
110	1.5	0	0	150
120	4.5	1	0	380

away. If you like regular Pringles more than regular potato chips, you will probably prefer the lighter Pringles as well. Half the tasters thought Reduced Fat Ruffles tasted good. The rest thought they tasted OK but wouldn't buy them again. Some tasters thought the Baked Lay's chips tasted good and said they would buy them again. Others thought they tasted OK and would not buy them again. I prefer the barbecue flavor over the regular just because it has more flavor going for it. Most of the tasters thought they would not buy the Mother's Potato Snaps again even though they tasted OK. It's really a cross between a cracker and a chip with a flaky texture and a lingering dried potato taste.

Chapter Six

Reduced-Fat Salad Dressing		Serving Size
★★1/2	Hidden Valley Ranch Light Original Ranch*	2 Tbsp.
★★1/2	Kraft 1/3 Less Fat Deliciously Right Ranch*	2 Tbsp.
★★1/2	Bernstein's Light Fantastic Creamy Dijon*	2 Tbsp.
★★	Newman's Own Light Italian	2 Tbsp.
★★	Kraft Deliciously Right 1000 Island	2 Tbsp.
★★	Bernstein's Light Fantastic Restaurant Ranch*	2 Tbsp.
★★	Bernstein's Light Fantastic Classico Italian	2 Tbsp.

* contains monosodium glutamate

Key: 4 stars=great!, 3=good, 2=OK, 1=skip it

Even regular calorie bottled salad dressings leave a lot to be desired, in my opinion. So finding a good tasting light or fat-free dressing might be described as mission impossible. I always thought if I tried every one of them I should be able to find a few good tasting ones. Well, this was my chance because that's exactly what we did for this book.

In the light salad dressing category, Hidden Valley Ranch Light Original Ranch was the best. Most tasters thought it tasted good or OK. Many tasters thought Kraft 1/3 Less Fat Deliciously Right Ranch tasted good or OK but a

Taste vs. Fat

Calories	Fat (g)	Saturated Fat (g)	Cholesterol (mg)	Sodium (mg)
80	7	0.5	0	270
110	11	2	10	310
50	1	0	0	310
20	0.5	0	0	380
70	4	1	5	320
35	0.5	0	5	240
40	1.5	0	0	300

couple didn't like its "packaged" flavor. Some tasters liked Bernstein's Light Fantastic Creamy Dijon and some thought it tasted OK, but many commented that it tasted too sweet. Newman's Own Light Italian was liked by a third of the tasters. A third thought it tasted OK, and a third threw it away. Most of the tasters thought Kraft Deliciously Right 1000 Island Dressing and Bernstein's Light Fantastic Restaurant Ranch tasted just OK, and complained of an odd flavor. I noticed a strong peppery flavor in the Bernstein's ranch dressing. Bernstein's Light Fantastic Classic

Reduced-Fat Salad Dressing (continued)

Italian has a strong vinegar and herb flavor but most tasters thought it tasted just OK and about a third said they would throw it away.

Helpful Hint: While perusing the salad dressing aisle looking for light or fat-free dressings, I found two dressings that are actually lower in fat than some of these, but you would never know it because their labels are devoid of any "light" or "reduced-fat" designations. Wish-Bone Olive Oil Vinaigrette tastes terrific and contains 5 grams of fat, mostly monounsaturated fat, per 2-table-

Fat-Free Salad Dressing		Serving Size
Blue Cheese:		
★★	Hidden Valley Ranch Fat Free Blue Cheese	2 Tbsp.
★	Kraft Free Blue Cheese	2 Tbsp.
Italian:		
★★1/2	Hidden Valley Ranch Fat Free Italian	2 Tbsp.
★★1/2	Kraft Free Italian	2 Tbsp.

Key: 4 stars=great!, 3=good, 2=OK, 1=skip it

spoon serving. Lawry's Red Wine Vinaigrette is also very pleasant tasting and contains 7 grams of fat per serving. Many of the people I surveyed for this book said that Girard's Caesar was their favorite salad dressing. I checked the label and it has a whopping 16 grams of fat per 2-tablespoon serving. But here's a way to bring it down to a more reasonable 8 grams of fat per serving: Blend 1/4 cup of this thick, intense-tasting dressing with 1/4 cup of water or lowfat milk. Now you have 1/2 cup of a thinner, milder dressing that contains 8 grams of fat per 2 tablespoons.

Calories	Fat (g)	Saturated Fat (g)	Cholesterol (mg)	Sodium (mg)
20	0	0	0	270
50	0	0	0	320
20	0	0	0	240
10	0	0	0	290

Chapter Six

Fat-Free Salad Dressing		Serving Size
Ranch:		
★★	Bernstein's Fat Free Creamy Herb Ranch	2 Tbsp.
★1/2	Kraft Free Peppercorn Ranch	2 Tbsp.
★1/2	Hidden Valley Ranch Fat Free Original Ranch	2 Tbsp.
★	Nalley's Fat Free Ranch	2 Tbsp.
★	Walden Farms Fat Free Ranch with Sun Dried Tomato	2 Tbsp.
Thousand Island:		
★★1/2	Nalley's Fat Free 1000 Island	2 Tbsp.
★1/2	Bernstein's Fat Free Rio Grande 1000 Island	2 Tbsp.
★1/2	Kraft Free Fat Free 1000 Island	2 Tbsp
★1/2	Wish-Bone Fat Free 1000 Island	2 Tbsp

Key: 4 stars=great!, 3=good, 2=OK, 1=skip it

Of the two fat-free blue cheese dressings we tasted, Hidden Valley Ranch Fat Free Blue Cheese is the better tasting—it had a more natural flavor. A third of the tasters thought it tasted good, a third thought it was OK, and a third threw it away. The Kraft Free Blue Cheese Dressing had a repulsive secondary taste. Most tasters said they would throw it away. Only a couple tasters thought it tasted OK.

Of the numerous fat-free Italian dressings, Hidden Valley Ranch Fat Free Italian and

Taste vs. Fat

Calories	Fat (g)	Saturated Fat (g)	Cholesterol (mg)	Sodium (mg)
30	0	0	0	340
50	0	0	0	360
45	0	0	0	320
40	0	0	0	240
25	0	0	0	290
30	0	0	0	210
40	0	0	0	290
45	0	0	0	300
35	0	0	0	290

Kraft Free Italian were both liked by almost half the tasters. A few thought they tasted OK and a few threw them away. The Kraft Free struck me as a good marinade because it has a strong vinegar and herb flavor.

There were no fat-free ranch dressings that anyone liked much. The top rated slot, inhabited by Bernstein's Fat Free Creamy Herb Ranch is more like the lesser of all evils. Most tasters thought it tasted OK. Some tasters thought Kraft Free Peppercorn Ranch and Hidden Valley Ranch

Chapter Six

Fat-Free Salad Dressing (continued)

Fat Free Original Ranch tasted OK but many more tasters threw them out. Everyone said they threw away Nalley's Fat Free Ranch and Walden Farms Fat Free Ranch with Sun-Dried Tomato, the latter of which had a very repulsive flavor to it—I repeat, repulsive.

If you are looking for simple tasting fat-free Thousand Island dressing, Nalley's Fat Free Thousand Island Dressing is the ticket. Most

Taste vs. Fat

tasters thought it tasted OK or good. If you want a fat-free Thousand Island dressing with a twist, then you might want to try Bernstein's Rio Grande Thousand Island Dressing. Half of the tasters thought this tasted OK; the other half threw it away. The same went for Kraft Free Thousand Island, which was a sweeter rendition of the dressing, and Wishbone Fat Free Thousand Island Dressing, which offers much stronger flavors than the other dressings.

Chapter Six

Sausage Links & Patties		Serving Size
★★★★	Jimmy Dean Light Sausage	75g (uncooked)
★★★★	Jones Light Pork and Rice Links	2 links (56g)
★★1/2	The Turkey Store Mild Breakfast Sausage Patties	2 patties (64g)
★★1/2	Butterball Lean Fresh Turkey Breakfast Sausage Links	2 links (57g)
★★	Healthy Choice Low Fat Breakfast Sausage (links and patties)	2 (45g)
★	Green Giant Breakfast Links	3 links (65g)
★	Morningstar Farms Breakfast Links or Patties	2 (45g)

Key: 4 stars=great!, 3=good, 2=OK, 1=skip it

After tasting all the sausage products, I kept wondering how I could have a sausage that tastes like the Jimmy Dean Light sausage but with a little less fat. At 14 grams of fat per serving, even the light version is a bit too high in fat. Jimmy Dean Light is still pretty greasy too—which can be a good or bad thing, depending on how you feel about grease. I came up with a way to make Jimmy Dean Light sausage a little lighter and less greasy—see the following Helpful Hint.

The two sausage favorites are Jimmy Dean Light, which tastes just like regular sausage, complete with some of the grease, and Jones Light

Taste vs. Fat

Calories	Fat (g)	Saturated Fat (g)	Cholesterol (mg)	Sodium (mg)
180	14	1	55	500
130	11	4	20	420
150	12	3	50	410
80	4.5	1.5	50	380
50	1.5	0.5	15	300
120	6	1	0	430
60	2.5	0.5	0	340

Pork and Rice Links. They both are by no means low fat, but they are great alternatives to the real thing—which is even higher in fat. Many tasters even liked the Jimmy Dean and Jones Light sausages better than regular sausage because they taste the same as real sausage but with less grease. Tasters thought the next two sausage selections, The Turkey Store Mild Breakfast Sausage and Butterball Lean Fresh Turkey Breakfast Sausage, tasted good or OK. Tasters had the same basic reaction to Healthy Choice Breakfast Sausage, although a few tasters didn't like it at all. I didn't like the texture very much. But the Green Giant

Chapter Six

Suasage Links and Patties (continued)

Breakfast Links and Morningstar Farms Breakfast Links were thrown out by just about everyone.

Helpful Hint: For a sausage that tastes almost as good as Jimmy Dean Light but is less greasy and

Smoked Sausage		Serving Size
★★★	Hillshire Farm Lite Smoked Sausage	2 oz
★★	Mr. Turkey Smoked Sausage	2 oz
★★	Healthy Choice Lowfat Smoked Sausage	2 oz

Key: 4 stars=great!, 3=good, 2=OK, 1=skip it

Hillshire Farms Lite Smoked Sausage has a greasier appearance and more of an animal-fat flavor than the others—which can make it more or less desirable depending on your preference. More tasters rated this as good. But there were still two families that rated this just OK and would not buy it again. Now here's where it gets complicated. Some of the tasters preferred Mr. Turkey Smoked

Taste vs. Fat

lower in fat, process half a pound of ground turkey breast with a 12-ounce package of Jimmy Dean Light in the food processor. Voila! Now you have a good tasting sausage with 114 calories, 7 grams of fat, .5 grams of saturated fat, and 42 milligrams of cholesterol per 1.5 ounces of cooked sausage.

Calories	Fat (g)	Saturated Fat (g)	Cholesterol (mg)	Sodium (mg)
120	8	4.5	25	510
90	5	2.5	30	600
70	1.5	0.5	25	480

Sausage to the Healthy Choice and some said they would buy the Healthy Choice sausage again over Mr. Turkey. And about half the tasters said they didn't like the Healthy Choice sausage while about a third didn't like the Mr. Turkey Smoked Sausage. So that's why the Mr. Turkey sausage is listed above Healthy Choice. Healthy Choice sausage is a tad milder.

Chapter Six

Snack Cakes	Serving Size
★★ Hostess Lights Twinkies	1 cake (43g)
★★ Hostess Lights Low Fat Cupcakes	1 cake (43g)

Key: 4 stars=great!, 3=good, 2=OK, 1=skip it

I am not honestly sure if my memory of what a regular Hostess Twinkie or Cupcake tastes like is truly accurate. I think things taste better when you're a kid peeking inside your lunch box to see what surprises await you. When I tasted the light versions of the Hostess Twinkie and Cupcake, I have to admit I was a little disappointed. They tasted all right, the Twinkie much better than the cupcake, but still not how I remembered them

Taste vs. Fat

Calories	Fat (g)	Saturated Fat (g)	Cholesterol (mg)	% Calories from sugar
130	1.5	0	0	49%
140	1.5	0	0	46%

tasting almost 30 years ago. Most of the tasters confirmed that these lighter versions left a lot to be desired. A few tasters thought they tasted good, but most thought they tasted OK or threw them away.

The original Twinkie contains 30 more calories and 3.5 grams more fat than the lighter version (of the same weight). The original Hostess Cupcake, weighing 7 grams more than the light cupcake, contains 40 more calories and 4.5 grams more fat.

Chapter Six

Soup	Serving Size
Chicken Noodle:	
★★★★ Campbell's Healthy Request Hearty Chicken Noodle	1 cup
★★★★ Progresso Healthy Classics Chicken Noodle	1 cup
★★ Healthy Choice Old Fashioned Chicken Noodle	1 cup
Minestrone:	
★★★ Healthy Choice Minestrone	1 cup
★★★ Progresso Healthy Classics Minestrone	1 cup
★★1/2 Campbell's Healthy Request Hearty Minestrone	1 cup
New England Clam Chowder:	
★★★★ Healthy Choice New England Clam Chowder	1 cup ready to eat
★★★ Campbell's Healthy Request New England Clam Chowder	1 cup
★ Progresso Healthy Classics New England Clam Chowder 99% Fat Free	1 cup ready to eat
Cream of Chicken or Mushroom:	
★★1/2 Campbell's Reduced Fat Cream of Mushroom	1/2 cup
★★1/2 Campbell's Reduced Fat Cream of Chicken	1/2 cup

Key: 4 stars=great!, 3=good, 2=OK, 1=skip it

I don't know too many people who don't have a couple cans of soup in their pantry just in case

Taste vs. Fat

Calories	Fat (g)	Saturated Fat (g)	Cholesterol (mg)	Sodium (mg)
160	3	1	20	480
80	2	0.5	20	480
140	3	1	10	400
110	1	0	0	390
120	2.5	0	0	510
120	2	0.5	0.5	480
120	1.5	1	10	480
110	3	1	10	480
120	2	0.5	5	530
70	3.5	0.5	5	940
80	4	1.5	15	950

someone gets the flu, or to go with a quick sandwich on a cold winter day. But all reduced-fat

Chapter Six

Soup (continued)

soups are not created equal, at least not in flavor. Some definitely taste better than others.

Both Campbell's Healthy Request Hearty Chicken Noodle and Progresso Healthy Classics Chicken Noodle had a nice, homemade taste. Many of the tasters thought they tasted great. The Healthy Choice Chicken Noodle had a bland taste.

Of the minestrone soups, Healthy Choice got my vote. It had a nicer flavor than the rest. Some tasters also liked Progresso Healthy Classics Minestrone. Most of the tasters thought Campbell's Healthy Request Hearty Minestrone tasted good or OK.

Most everyone liked Healthy Choice's New England Clam Chowder the best. It had a

Taste vs. Fat

strong pepper taste compared with the other high-scoring clam chowder, Campbell's Healthy Request, which had a little less flavor than Healthy Choice. Both clam chowders were nice and chunky compared with Progresso Healthy Classics New England Clam Chowder, which had a bland flavor and totally unappealing texture. I actually threw most of it out.

Campbell's has come out with reduced-fat versions of their condensed cream of mushroom and chicken soups. Most tasters thought they worked fine in their mixed dishes and casseroles, but a few tasters thought they weren't as good as the regular versions, and they probably wouldn't buy them again.

Chapter Six

Sour Cream	Serving Size
★★★1/2 Naturally Yours Fat Free	2 Tbsp.
★★ Lucerne Light	2 Tbsp.
★★ Knudsen Light	2 Tbsp.
★ Knudsen Free	2 Tbsp.

Key: 4 stars=great!, 3=good, 2=OK, 1=skip it

The best tasting sour cream is a fat-free sour cream, not a light sour cream—amazing, but true. I started using Naturally Yours Fat Free in the cow-hide package (white with black spots) months before I started working on this book. At the time I was surprised that I liked it, since I had detested every other fat-free sour cream. I learned you can't really make a blanket statement, like "all fat-free sour creams don't taste very good," because they all may taste a little different. Most

Taste vs. Fat

Calories	Fat (g)	Saturated Fat (g)	Cholesterol (mg)	Sodium (mg)
20	0	0	0	50
30	2	1	10	50
40	2.5	2	10	20
35	0	0	<5	25

tasters thought Naturally Yours Fat Free's taste and texture were good or great. It was the only light or fat-free sour cream that one family liked. Some tasters thought Lucerne Light and Knudsen Light tasted just OK and some thought they tasted good or great. The taste and texture of Lucerne Light was more like plain yogurt than sour cream, and Knudsen Light tasted a bit too sour for my liking. Knudsen Free had an undesirable taste and texture. Most of the tasters threw it away.

Chapter Six

Tortilla Chips		Serving Size
★★1/2	Doritos Reduced Fat Nacho Cheesier	13 chips (28g)
★★1/2	R.W. Garcia Natural	15 chips (30g)
★★	Guiltless Gourmet Chili & Lime	20 chips (28g)
★★	Baked Tostitos	13 chips (28g)

Key: 4 stars=great!, 3=good, 2=OK, 1=skip it

Fat-free or baked tortilla chips came up several times in my survey of products people had tried that tasted terrible. I personally rate fat-free tortilla chips right up there with cardboard. Maybe it takes more like 4 grams of fat to make a decent tasting tortilla chip, because most of the tasters liked Doritos new Reduced Fat Nacho Cheesier Chips. My family loves them. But if you like your tortilla chips without a thick coating of spicy orange powder, you might want to try R.W. Garcia Natural Tortilla Chips; most of the tasters thought they tasted good and would buy them again.

Taste vs. Fat

Calories	Fat (g)	Saturated Fat (g)	Cholesterol (mg)	Sodium (mg)
130	5	1	0	210
140	4	0.5	0	45
110	1	0	0	200
110	1	0	0	140

About a fourth of the tasters thought they tasted OK and would not buy them again. Some tasters thought they needed more salt or more flavor.

I was surprised how good the Guiltless Gourmet Chili & Lime Chips tasted. They seemed to have a better texture than the Baked Tostitos, and they definitely had more flavor. One third of the tasters thought they tasted like cardboard and two-thirds thought they tasted OK. One family thought they tasted good. Only one family thought the Baked Tostitos tasted good and said they would buy them again.

Chapter Six

Weight Watchers Breakfast On-the-Go		Serving Size
★★★	Sausage Biscuit	1 (85g)
★★1/2	English Muffin Sandwich	1 (113g)

Weight Watchers Breakfast Breads		Serving Size
★★1/2	Fat Free Blueberry Muffins	1 (71g)
★★1/2	Glazed Cinnamon Rolls	1 (59g)

Key: 4 stars=great!, 3=good, 2=OK, 1=skip it

We tasted some of the Weight Watchers breakfast line in case you occasionally like a microwavable breakfast. I did, however, limit the testing to those with 40 percent calories from sugar or less. The Sausage Biscuit tasted pretty good. Even though it contains 50 percent less fat than regular breakfast

Taste vs. Fat

Calories	Fat (g)	Saturated Fat (g)	Cholesterol (mg)	Sodium (mg)
230	11	3.5	25	660
210	5	3	20	420

Calories	Fat (g)	Saturated Fat (g)	Cholesterol (mg)	% Calories from sugar
160	0	0	0	37.5%
200	5	1.5	5	20%

sandwiches, it still contains 43 percent calories from fat. Half the tasters thought the English Muffin Sandwich tasted good and half thought it tasted OK. Some tasters thought the Fat Free Blueberry Muffins and Glazed Cinnamon Rolls tasted good and some thought they tasted just OK.

Chapter Six

Weight Watchers Desserts		Serving Size
★★★	Chocolate Eclair	1 (59g)
★★★	New York Style Cheesecake with black cherry swirl	1 (70g)
★★	Chocolate Mousse	1 (77g)

Key: 4 stars=great!, 3=good, 2=OK, 1=skip it

I also decided to try Weight Watchers desserts, at least those with the least amount of sugar and calories. What Weight Watchers is really selling you here is portion control. They portion out really small servings of fairly reduced-fat items (still reasonably high in calories, though, considering the small serving size), wrap them in plastic, put them in colorful boxes, and charge you an arm and a leg. But I know some people really love

Taste vs. Fat

Calories	Fat (g)	Saturated Fat (g)	Cholesterol (mg)	% Calories from sugar
150	4	1	30	37%
150	5	2	10	45%
190	4	1.5	5	13%

this service because my own mother recommended the cheesecake to me. The problem is, some people will want to eat the whole box, containing two mini cheesecakes, and that's 300 calories and 10 grams of fat. The Chocolate Eclair and the New York Style Cheesecake taste pretty darn good. The Chocolate Mousse tastes OK. One family thought it tasted great.

Chapter Six

Whipped Topping	Serving Size
★★★ Cool Whip Lite	2 Tbsp.
★★1/2 Cool Whip Free	2 Tbsp.
★★ Dream Whip Whipped Topping Mix*	2 Tbsp.
★1/2 Kraft Free Fat Free Whipped Topping	2 Tbsp.

*prepared with low-fat milk and vanilla extract

Key: 4 stars=great!, 3=good, 2=OK, 1=skip it

Cool Whip Lite is one of those "whatever you grew up with" things. If you grew up with only real whipped cream, chances are you turn up your nose to synthetic whipped toppings that come in tubs and hold their shape even when left at room temperature for several hours. While I prefer the taste of whipped cream, Cool Whip Lite comes in handy when I need something similar with less fat and many of the tasters like it and already use it. Several tasters thought the new fat-free Cool Whip tasted pretty good. I didn't mind it at first, but the more I tasted it, the more it seemed to

Taste vs. Fat

Calories	Fat (g)	Saturated Fat (g)	Cholesterol (mg)	% Calories from sugar
20	1	1	0	20%
15	0	0	0	26%
20	0.5	0.5	0	40%
15	0	0	0	53%

have a strange aftertaste. Many of the tasters thought it would work best mixed with something like pudding or yogurt.

Dream Whip tasted OK. I don't mind using it in some recipes, but it has a very different flavor than real whipped cream. Kraft Free Fat Free Whipped Topping tastes OK, and that's being generous. The texture is glossy like a meringue and the first four ingredients are water, dextrose, sugar, and nonfat milk solids. None of the tasters thought they would buy this product again.

Chapter Six

Low-Fat Yogurt		Serving Size
★★★★	Dannon Double Delights Bavarian Cream with Raspberry Topping	6 oz
★★★	Yoplait Lowfat Strawberry	6 oz
★★1/2	Dannon Lowfat Strawberry Fruit on the Bottom	8 oz

Key: 4 stars=great!, 3=good, 2=OK, 1=skip it

What's red and white and tastes so delicious it's more like a dessert? Dannon Double Delights Bavarian Cream with Raspberry Topping. This yogurt tops our list of low-fat yogurts, which we limited to strawberry or raspberry flavors. Everyone who tried the Bavarian Cream liked it.

Taste vs. Fat

Calories	Fat (g)	Saturated Fat (g)	Cholesterol (mg)	% Calories from sugar
170	2.5	1.5	10	66%
180	1.5	1	10	60%
240	3	1.5	15	73%

Tasters also liked Yoplait's Lowfat Strawberry Yogurt. All tasters rated it as good or great. Half the tasters thought the Dannon Lowfat Strawberry Fruit On the Bottom tasted good. The rest thought it tasted OK. The strawberry flavor wasn't as strong as the Yoplait.

Chapter Six

Fat-Free Yogurt		Serving Size
★★★	Continental Nonfat Lemon	1 cup
★★★	SnackWell's Double Chocolate	3/4 cup
★★1/2	Yoplait Light Fat Free Strawberry (with Nutrasweet)	6 oz
★★	Dannon Light Fat Free Strawberry (with Nutrasweet)	8 oz

Key: 4 stars=great!, 3=good, 2=OK, 1=skip it

It's hard to find a fat-free yogurt that isn't made with NutraSweet. Yogurts made with NutraSweet tend to have an unappealing secondary flavor. I did find a couple yogurts that used plain old sugar, and ironically they happen to be at the top of the list. Continental Nonfat Yogurt had a good flavor and texture. I was surprised I liked the SnackWell's Double Chocolate Yogurt. Who else but SnackWell's would think of putting chocolate and

Taste vs. Fat

Calories	Fat (g)	Saturated Fat (g)	Cholesterol (mg)	% Calories from sugar
190	0	0	5	51%
190	0	0	<5	63%
90	0	0	<5	36%
100	0	0	<5	56%

yogurt together. More than half the tasters thought it tasted good, and the rest thought it tasted OK. Tasters rated Yoplait Light Fat Free Strawberry about the same as the SnackWell's yogurt. Most of the tasters thought Dannon Light Fat Free Strawberry Yogurt tasted OK. One family thought it tasted good. Many tasters noticed an aftertaste with the Yoplait Light and the Dannon Light.

Chapter Six

CHAPTER SEVEN
Buried Treasures

Taste vs. Fat

Chapter Seven

Taste vs. Fat

The products listed in this chapter are the diamonds in the rough. They are really good products that you may not have noticed among the thousands and thousands of other products trying to grab your attention in the grocery store. Needless to say, with all the new food products being pumped onto the supermarket shelves and advertising slogans and nutrition buzzwords radiating from every food package, a simple grocery trip can feel more like a jungle safari.

Fortunately, there are a few buried treasures waiting to be discovered. For example, I would never have even seen the delicious Kosher brand Chicken Breast Nuggets, which turned out to be the lowest-fat frozen chicken nugget on the market, if not for a box that happened to be in the wrong place.

Lower-fat chicken nuggets may not mean anything to you, but take my word for it, a bag in the freezer comes in handy when you make something like crab crepes for you and your spouse—a dinner guaranteed to turn any toddler's nose up. Granted, by no means are they low fat, but they do have the least amount of fat of any other frozen chicken or turkey nugget, and the kids love them (they are best baked in the oven).

I try to remain open-minded when it comes to trying new foods, but up until now I've never tasted a nonmeat burger that I've even remotely liked (including Green Giant's veggie burger in the frozen food section). Then I tried The Original Gardenburger, both in a restaurant and subsequently from the frozen food section of my local supermarket—finally, a vegetarian burger I didn't have to spit out. I even detected a hint of artichoke heart flavor (which, according to the ingredient list, is not in there).

The point is, The Original Gardenburger was a surprising find for me. There is a subtle "nice" vegetable flavor to it, one I definitely wouldn't mind having again. Mind you, I'm not sure this would go over with your basic beef-loving crowd of men—but it's a good bet for people who like eating vegetarian as often as possible.

Now for other buried treasures.

Sara Lee Reduced Fat Apple Pie

This pie appeared in supermarkets right before this book came out, so few people had time to taste it. Still, most everyone thought it tasted good or OK. The taste was similar to a regular frozen pie, except the crust wasn't quite as flaky.

Serving Size: 1/6 pie (128 g)
Calories: 290 • Fat (g): 8 • Saturated Fat (g): 1.5
Cholesterol (mg): <5 • Sodium (mg): 400

Stella d'Oro Breadsticks

These breadsticks are a nice addition to lunch boxes or family picnics.

Serving Size: 1 stick
Calories: 40 • Fat (g): 1 • Saturated Fat (g): 0
Cholesterol (mg): 0 • Sodium (mg): 40

Bugles Light 60% Less Fat

I remember Bugles fondly from my youth. I liked them then—and I like the lower-fat Bugles now. Half the tasters thought they tasted good and half said they tasted OK.

Serving Size: 1 1/2 cups
Calories: 130 • Fat (g): 2.5 • Saturated Fat (g): 0.5
Cholesterol (mg): 0 • Sodium (mg): 380

I Can't Believe It's Not Butter Spray

Once I got past the idea of a butter spray, I tried this product on bread and vegetables. I have to admit it tasted pretty good on certain things. Since the first ingredient is water, it would tend to make certain foods soggy if applied generously, as is the case with popcorn. Some of the tasters liked using this for certain foods, and some just aren't the butter-in-a-spray-bottle type. But we've certainly come a long way since the packets of gummy Butter Buds from years past.

Serving Size: 4 sprays
Calories: 0 • Fat (g): 0 • Saturated Fat (g): 0
Cholesterol (mg): 0 • Sodium (mg): 15

Chapter Seven

Sara Lee Reduced Fat Original Cream Cheesecake

If every little bit counts, then maybe this new reduced-fat cheesecake is worthwhile. It contains 25 percent less fat than the original version, but every taster thought it tasted terrific—they couldn't taste a difference.

Serving Size: 1/4 cheesecake (120g)
Calories: 310 • Fat (g): 13 • Saturated Fat (g): 8
Cholesterol (mg): 70 • Calories from Sugar: 70%

Chicken Breast Nuggets

My family loves the Empire Kosher Chicken Breast Nuggets. They are tender and tasty. Safeway Select Breaded Chicken Breast Nuggets also will probably go over with even particularly picky palates under the age of 5. These nuggets taste best baked in the oven, but if you're in a pinch you can microwave them or broil them, turning often and checking constantly.

I couldn't help but notice that the Empire Kosher product didn't contain a long list of additives and preservatives. That's a real plus for me and for most mothers I know.

Serving Size: 5 Safeway Select nuggets (85g)
Calories: 200 • Fat (g): 10 • Saturated Fat (g): 2
Cholesterol (mg): 45 • Sodium (mg): 610
Serving Size: 5 Empire Kosher nuggets (92g)
Calories: 180 • Fat (g): 9 • Saturated Fat (g): 1.5
Cholesterol (mg): 15 • Sodium (mg): 370

Taste vs. Fat

Asian Favorites Cashew Chicken

This is a quick dinner in a pinch. You can make it with only 1 tablespoon of oil instead of 2 using a good nonstick fry pan. I use 3 chicken breasts instead of 4, and 3 carrots instead of 2. Preparing it this way gives you a 25-percent-calories-from-fat entrée.

Serving Size: Libby's Asian Favorites Cashew Chicken dinner kit, prepared with 3 chicken breasts, 1 Tbsp. oil, 3 celery stalks and 3 carrots, chopped.

Calories: 416 • Fat (g): 11.5 • Saturated Fat (g): 2
Cholesterol (mg): 51 • Sodium (mg): 703

Hershey's Reduced Fat Chocolate Chips

These new chips have a very similar flavor to semi-sweet chocolate chips. The texture seemed less smooth and creamy to me, though. This new product contains Salatrim fat, only 55 percent of which is used by the body. Some tasters thought these tasted good (not much of a difference from regular chocolate chips) and others thought they tasted OK. For comparison purposes, one tablespoon of Hershey's regular semi-sweet chips contains 70 calories and 4 grams of fat.

Serving Size: 1 Tbsp.
Calories: 60 • Fat (g): 2 • Saturated Fat (g): 2
Cholesterol (mg): 0 • Calories from Sugar: 60%

Chapter Seven

Sara Lee Reduced Fat Cheese Coffee Cake

This tasted pretty good to the few people who got a chance to try it. It had a nice flavor and texture. I only wish it had more "cheese" to it.

Serving Size: 1/6 pie (54 g)
Calories: 180 • Fat (g): 6 • Saturated Fat (g): 1.5
Cholesterol (mg): 20 • Sodium (mg): 230

Marie Calendar's Reduced Fat Croutons

You can find these gourmet croutons in the produce section of most supermarkets. They come in several flavors, such as savory garlic and Parmesan. They work pretty well in salads and casseroles. These croutons have 25 percent less fat and, for the most part, taste like regular croutons.

Serving Size: 2 Tbsp.
Calories: 30 • Fat (g): 1 • Saturated Fat (g): 0
Cholesterol (mg): 0 • Sodium (mg): 80

Keebler Reduced Fat Graham Cracker Ready Crust

I barely noticed a difference between this crust and the regular ready-made graham cracker crust.

Serving Size: 1/8 crust
Calories: 100 • Fat (g): 3 • Saturated Fat (g): 1
Cholesterol (mg): 0 • Calories from Sugar: 28%

Taste vs. Fat

Eagle Brand Sweetened Condensed Skimmed Milk

I was literally jumping in the aisles when I saw this new product. So many times I've wished for a less-fat sweetened condensed product to use as a substitute in recipes (even fudge). I've tried this product in several different types of recipes and it worked well as a substitute for regular sweetened condensed milk. It contains fewer calories than regular sweetened condensed milk, which contains 123 calories and 3.3 grams of fat per 2 tablespoons.

Serving Size: 2 Tbsp.
Calories: 110 • Fat (g): 0 • Saturated Fat (g): 0
Cholesterol (mg): <5 • Calories from Sugar: 87%

Sara Lee Reduced Fat Pound Cake

Now don't get all excited. This pound cake has only 35 percent less fat than the original version, which means one-fourth of the pound cake (a rather large portion) still contains 11 grams of fat along with 280 calories. Most tasters thought it tasted pretty good, but not great. The cake would probably work well if something was added to it, such as fresh berries and Light Cool Whip.

Serving Size: 1/4 pie (76 g)
Calories: 280 • Fat (g): 11 • Saturated Fat (g): 3
Cholesterol (mg): 65 • Calories from Sugar: 37%

Chapter Seven

Vidalia O's Onion Rings

My husband and I have quite a few favorite foods in common—onion rings is one of them. I was content to order them once a year at a restaurant, and then I found Vidalia O's by Bland Farms quite by accident. After reading the labels of the other neighboring frozen onion ring brands, I quickly discovered this new brand has a lot less fat. It has a beer batter type breading instead of the crumb type breading, which I personally prefer. My only advice is to buy more than one box, since they are so good and one box only contains about 12 rings.

Follow the directions on the box for baking the onion rings. It takes just 15 minutes at 400°.

Serving Size: 6 rings (84g)
Calories: 180 • Fat (g): 7 • Saturated Fat (g): 4
Cholesterol (mg): 5 • Sodium (mg): 200

Wolfgang Puck's Fat-Free Grilled Vegetable Cheeseless Frozen Pizza

A pizza fan, I truly am—but a frozen pizza fan, I am not. I've tried a few of the lower-fat pizzas on the market and was not impressed mostly because of their choice in reduced-fat cheese, or the sheer lack of cheese. So the idea of a cheeseless grilled vegetable pizza caught my eye. This way, you can add the reduced-fat cheese of your choice in the amount of your choice.

I used a mixture of Cracker Barrel Light

Sharp Cheddar, Parmesan cheese, and part-skim mozzarella. This will add about 90 calories, 6 grams of fat (4 grams of which are saturated), 20 milligrams of cholesterol, and 240 milligrams of sodium to 1 serving of pizza (one half of a whole) if you add 1/2 cup of the grated mixture on top of the pizza.
Serving Size: 1/2 pizza
Calories: 200 • Fat (g): 0 • Saturated Fat (g): 0
Cholesterol (mg): 0 • Sodium (mg): 430

Snyder's of Hanover Fat Free Mini Pretzels

Granted, pretzels are already very low in fat. So making fat-free pretzels really isn't going to help Americans lower their total fat intake by leaps and bounds. But, if you are interested in fat-free pretzels, this brand, in particular, is a tasty option. It also happens to have less sodium per serving than other fat-free pretzels.
Serving Size: 20 minis (30g)
Calories: 110 • Fat (g): 0 • Saturated Fat (g): 0
Cholesterol (mg): 0 • Sodium (mg): 250

Rosarita No Fat Refried Beans

What could be easier than opening a can of tasty refried beans to complement any Mexican meal. Every taster said they would definitely buy this again, and a few of the tasters were already regular purchasers of the Rosarita No Fat Zesty Salsa Refried Beans. You can't go wrong with this product. You get

a tasty bean dish with no fat and more fiber (5 grams per 1/2 cup) than you'll know what to do with.
Serving Size: 1/2 cup
Calories: 100 • Fat (g): 0 • Saturated Fat (g): 0
Cholesterol (mg): 0 • Sodium (mg): 670

Mahatma Spanish Rice

This is truly a great tasting Spanish rice. It does contains MSG and sodium bisulfite, however. The nutrition information given on the label (0.5 grams of fat and 180 calories) does not include the tablespoon of margarine called for in the directions. Tricky, aren't they? I used 1 1/2 teaspoons of canola oil instead of 1 tablespoon of margarine, and it turned out terrific.
Serving Size: 1/3 cup rice mix + 1 Tbsp. seasoning
Calories: 180 • Fat (g): 0.5* • Saturated Fat (g): 0
Cholesterol (mg): 0 • Sodium (mg): 760
* This amount doesn't include any oil or margarine.

Vegetarian Burgers

I prefer the Original Gardenburger. It has an interesting flavor and texture. But if you're looking for a nonmeat burger that tastes like meat—then the Boca Burger is probably the ticket. As for the vegetable burgers marketed by Green Giant or Morningstar Farms? Don't ask—it ain't pretty.

The Boca Burger won a taste test of nonmeat burgers on the "Leeza" show. This burger tastes and feels more like a beef burger compared to the

Taste vs. Fat

Gardenburger. It is made from soy protein, potato starch, soy fiber, dehydrated onion, spices, carrageenan, garlic and natural malt extract. I served one of these burgers to a good friend of mine and she really liked it. But when I asked her if her husband would like it, she answered a definitive "no" without hesitation.

The Original Gardenburger and the Boca Burger both bring with them a big bonus—fiber. The Boca Burger contains 4 grams of fiber and the Gardenburger has 5 grams.

Helpful Hint: Pan-fry either burger listed above with 1/2 teaspoon of oil or spray both sides generously with no-stick cooking spray. I particularly like serving the Gardenburger with sautéed mushrooms and a slice of reduced-fat garlic-Jack or Monterey Jack cheese. I like to serve the Boca Burger with lettuce, tomato, a slice of Cracker Barrel Light Sharp Cheddar, and a squirt of a light Thousand Island dressing. Watch out, McDonald's!

Serving Size: 1 Gardenburger (71g)
Calories: 140 • Fat (g): 2.5 • Saturated Fat (g): 0.5
Cholesterol (mg): 5 • Sodium (mg): 180

Serving Size: 1 Boca Burger (71g)
Calories: 110 • Fat (g): 2 • Saturated Fat (g): 0.5
Cholesterol (mg): 3 • Sodium (mg): 296

Chapter Seven

Adding Less Fat to New & Popular Mixes

I never let a little thing like package directions get in the way of making something lower in fat. Call me cocky, but I always carefully read the package directions only to change them—usually to reduce the fat and calories. Sometimes it works out better than other times. The products listed below turned out great, in spite of my lower-fat efforts.

Betty Crocker Sunkist Lemon Poppy Seed Muffin Mix prepared with 1 Tbsp. oil, 3 Tbsp. fat-free sour cream, 1 egg or 1/4 cup egg substitute, and 1 cup water
Serving Size: 1/12th
Calories: 156 • Fat (g): 3.5 • Saturated Fat (g): 0.7
Cholesterol (mg): 17 • Calories from Sugar: 38%

Betty Crocker (100% Real Idaho Potatoes) Homestyle Cheesy Scalloped Potatoes made with 1 Tbsp. margarine instead of 2 Tbsp., and 3/4 cup low-fat milk instead of 2/3 cup whole milk. Contains sodium sulfite and bisulfite.
Serving Size: 1/5th
Calories: 125 • Fat (g): 4 • Saturated Fat (g): 1.5
Cholesterol (mg): 7 • Sodium (mg) 532

JELL-O No Bake Double Layer Lemon Dessert Make the crust with 3 Tbsp. honey, 1 Tbsp. melted margarine, and 1 Tbsp. milk instead of 2 Tbsp. sugar

Taste vs. Fat

and 1/3 cup melted margarine. And make the filling with 1% milk instead of 2%.

Serving Size: 1/8 package

Calories: 218 • Fat (g): 5.5 • Saturated Fat (g): 2.5
Cholesterol (mg): 2 • Calories from Sugar: 48%

Chapter Seven

Index

Taste vs. Fat

Index

additives, food, 12-14
bacon, 62-63
baking mixes, 25-29, 64-65, 190-191
beans, refried, 187-188
breadsticks, 181
breakfast bars, 140-141
brownie mixes, 64-65
brownies, packaged, 66-67
butter spray, 181
butter, light, 130-131
cake mixes, 68-69
cake,
    cheese, 182
    coffee, 184
    pound, 185
cakes, snack, 156-157
calories, 23
    fat and, 4-5, 10-11, 21-25
candy, 70-71
caramel corn, 72-73
cheese puffs, 80-81
cheese,
    cream, 102-103
    fat-free, 78-79
    reduced-fat, 74-77
cheesecake, 182
chicken dinner, 183
chicken nuggets, 182
chili, canned, 80-81

Taste vs. Fat

chips,
- potato, 142-143
- tortilla, 164-165

chocolate chips, 183

cholesterol,
- blood, 14-15
- dietary, 15-16
- fat and, 15

cinnamon rolls, 82-83

coffee cake, 184

cold cuts, 84-87

condensed milk, 185

cookies, 24
- fat-free, 88-91
- low-fat, 92-97

crackers, 98-103

cream cheese, 102-103

crescent rolls, 104-105

croutons, 184

crust, pie, 184

dieting, 11

doughnuts, 104-105

dressings, salad,
- fat-free, 146-151
- reduced-fat, 144-147

egg substitutes, 106-107

entrée, frozen, 110-113

fat,
- calories and, 4-5, 10-11, 21-25
- taste and, 39-42, 44-47

Index

fats, dietary, definitions of, 16-18
food additives, 12-14
frosting, 108-109
frozen entrées, 110-113
granola bars, 114-115
hot dogs and franks, 116-117
ice cream bars, 126-127
ice cream toppings, 128-129
ice cream,
    fat-free, 124-125
    light, 118-121
lipid, definition of, 16
margarine,
    diet, 130-131
    fat-free, 47
mayonnaise, 132-135
meat, luncheon, 84-87
mixes,
    baking, 25-29, 64-65, 68-69, 134-135, 190-191
muffin mixes, 134-135, 190
nutrition terms, definitions of, 12
onion rings, 186
pancake mixes, 136-137
peanut butter, 138-139
pie crust, 184
pie, apple, 180
pizza, frozen, 186-187
pop-tarts, 140-141
popcorn, microwave, 138-139
portions, 21

potato chips, 142-143
potatoes, scalloped, 190
pound cake, 185
pretzels, 187
refried beans, 187-188
rice, Spanish, 188
rolls, crescent, 104-105
sausage links, 152-155
sausage patties, 152-155
sausage, smoked, 154-155
serving sizes, 21
shopping, food, 30-31
smoking, taste and, 51
snack bars, 140-141
snack cakes, 156-157
snack chips, 181
soup, 158-161
sour cream, 162-163
sugar, 23
taste, factors affecting, 36-42, 44-47, 51
topping, whipped, 170-171
tortilla chips, 164-165
vegetarian burgers, 179-180, 188-189
waffle mixes, 136-137
Weight Watchers products, 166-169
weight gain, national statistics, 9
whipped topping, 170-171
yogurt, fat-free, 174-175

Index

yogurt, frozen,
- fat-free, 122-123
- low-fat, 124-125

yogurt, low-fat, 172-173